DECOLONIZE HIPSTERS

Forthcoming from *Decolonize That! Handbooks for the Revolutionary Overthrow of Embedded Colonial Ideas*
Edited by Bhakti Shringarpure

DECOLONIZE
HIPSTERS

GRÉGORY PIERROT

OR Books

New York · London

The *Decolonize That!* series is produced in collaboration with *Warscapes* magazine.

Published by OR Books, New York and London
Visit our website at www.orbooks.com

Lyrics from "Merchandise" by Fugazi excerpted with permission from Ian MacKaye.

All rights information: rights@orbooks.com

First printing 2022

Cataloging-in-Publication data is available from the Library of Congress.
A catalog record for this book is available from the British Library.

paperback ISBN 978-1-68219-317-4 • ebook ISBN 978-1-68219-376-1

CONTENTS

EDITOR'S PREFACE

Why would the first book of the series *Decolonize That! Handbooks for the Revolutionary Overthrow of Embedded Colonial Ideas* take a shot at hipsters? How can white youth in skinny jeans and ironic t-shirts attempting to recycle mason jars and brew decent craft beer be held responsible for colonialism? If anything, hipsters are associated with progressive values and for attempting to carve a space outside of the cultural and economic mainstream. You're probably thinking it's because hipsters are now associated with capitalism. The twenty-first-century hipster has unabashedly allowed the hipster lifestyle to turn into a marketable and profitable brand. In fact, the hipster aesthetic has become not just a panty cut, but also a cocktail, a succulent, a set of fonts, and also, weirdly, a bunch of food items (think pickling). We bump into hipster lifestyle elements so frequently that we no longer recall their supposedly progressive beginnings.

Sure, consuming mainstreamed white culture in slick and "cool" packaging is definitely a big part of the problem, but that's not really what *Decolonize Hipsters* is about. In his fierce, funny and sometimes shocking book, Grégory Pierrot takes a deep dive into gentrification, cultural appropriation, and white supremacy, all undergirded by the one thing most dear to him: music. More importantly, he forces the reader to reckon with that tiresome thing: history. And by history, I mean colonial history.

Greg's book begins in the hipster heartland: Portland, Oregon. He finds himself part of the most Portlandian of all activities: a birdwatching event called Swift Watch where people gather to watch over a thousand types of migrating birds. Looking around, Greg realizes quite suddenly that he's the only Black man amidst a sea of "tattooed, fit, casually but smartly dressed, sun-kissed, cool" white folk. A fairly banal epiphany—"Why is Portland so fucking white?"— unleashes a hell ride in which histories of slavery, jazz, punk rock, cool-hunting, bohemian art, and fascist hairstyles come together to paint a new portrait of white culture.

A singularly important intervention in the book is Greg's ability to trace the history of hipsters to the histories of appropriating cultures born out of transatlantic slavery. The "history of hipsters is a not-so-secret history of race in the Atlantic world," he writes, revealing the fetish for all things Black and creole, whether it was music, dances, or dresses that were mimicked and appropriated by white bohemians on both sides of the Atlantic and transformed into what we've come to see as cool and hip. No surprise, then, that one of the iconic texts on this topic is Norman Mailer's 1957 essay "The White Negro: Superficial Reflections on the Hipster," which despite the ghastly title manages to get to a nugget of truth: that hipsterdom is all about chasing after Blackness, and is inevitably just as vague, extractive, and racist as that sounds.

Decolonize Hipsters is unsparing; perhaps that should be true of any decolonial project. Mostly, it refuses to cut any slack to the smug white progressive whose inclination towards narcissism and self-indulgent wokeness can often ring hollow in the face of activism towards anti-racism and militant feminism. As #decolonize becomes . . . well, hip, and has today alone yielded a half-million tags on Instagram, a rap on some white hipsters' knuckles is much needed. There is no one more ubiquitous than a hipster, and no bigger irony than a history that insists on being seen as radical and progressive while relying so much on an all-powerful, all-encompassing whiteness. For those puzzled at the current rise of white supremacy or the ascendance of the Proud Boys, or if you've wondered who exactly were those bearded, costumed and armed men attacking the Capitol on January 6, 2021, Greg's book shows that those undercurrents have been there all along, and live dangerously on through hipster fashion, retro hairdos, callous gentrification, and shameless appropriation.

What makes this book so special is Greg's easy fusion of his professorial expertise in nineteenth-century African American and Caribbean studies with fluency in music and popular culture. Sharp and stylish, the book doesn't hesitate to draw from hilarious personal anecdotes, many of which take place in Greg's native France, revealing that classy and bohemian Europe is no beacon of progress. The book's ability to link this unusual phenomenon with a toxic coloniality that we've ended up absorbing so unthinkingly makes it revolutionary. It is not merely timely, but head-turning, making us rethink, undo, unlearn, decenter, decolonize—the perfect way to launch the *Decolonize That!* series, which was conceived to solidify, declutter, and engage the push towards "decolonization" that is returning with a vengeance today.

Our new century has been marked by global mass mobilization for social justice, with the Arab Spring, the Movement for Black Lives, #MeToo, #FeesMustFall and Antifa signaling a strong desire and motivation to work towards overhauling social, political, cultural, economic, and institutional structures perceived as hegemonic, discriminatory, and oppressive. Evolving in tandem with these large social movements are smaller and less visible cultural shifts playing a significant role in shaping these movements, often providing them with politically coherent and historically grounded direction. The most prominent among these include the debates around decolonizing education in universities in Europe and the United States; the 2018 report released in France blowing the whistle on the historical theft of the thousands of African artifacts displayed in their museums; and lastly, the campaigns to raise awareness about the histories of violence and displacement of Indigenous peoples elided by American holidays such as Columbus Day and Thanksgiving.

Only recently, US President-elect Joe Biden expressly announced in his victory speech that the eradication of systemic racism is on the top of his agenda. Vice President-elect Kamala Harris echoed this sentiment and cited her distinction as the first woman and first person of color to serve in this position as a clear illustration of how sincere and serious they are about race. The American public has slowly started to embrace what would have been unacceptable only a couple of decades ago: confrontational women of color in positions of national leadership, such as "the Squad," as they are popularly called. The *Decolonize That!* series is a testament to our changing times and a rigorous attempt to bolster these shifts with the production of new knowledge about our society through the prism of "decolonization," a term that is at least seventy-five years old and grounded in Third Worldist struggles against colonialism. Yet, these ideas remain urgent because coloniality never really went away; it just morphed and mutated, or worse, we got used to it.

The #decolonize imperative surrounds us now, whether popping up in all kinds of diversity initiatives at institutions or part of the daily, micro-rebellious activism proliferating in memes and social media posts. At best, the hashtag #decolonize exposes a hunger for intellectual and ethical instruction on how to lead conscientious and balanced lives on a planet in environmental, economic, and political crisis. At worst, the #decolonize movement becomes ubiquitous and inchoate as the term becomes increasingly popular. What is most important is that a majority of us are realizing that coloniality has seeped into all aspects of our lives and is a deterrent to our very freedom. The books in this series are, indeed, handbooks helping us deconstruct what lays in the way of our freedom. They expose the role of hyper-capitalist consumption, stubborn patriotism, structural racism, misogyny, and a penchant for able-bodied exceptionalism in everything we participate in, whether it's yoga and meditation, fashion, what we read, or all that conscientious recycling (stay tuned for coming editions!).

Reading the books in this series will, perhaps, involve a scary look in the mirror, but remember, we are all in this together. We are building a better future. So, go ahead, decolonize everything!

—Bhakti Shringarpure
January 2021

INTRODUCTION

Dig, if you will, the picture: it was 2014, and I was visiting Portland, Oregon, for the first time ever. Now mind you, I had been to the Pacific Northwest before, and if we're going to be honest (and we are, aren't we?), the area had occupied a special place in my heart and soul since high school. I was a teenager in the nineties, you see, when Seattle seemed a rainy, foggy, exotic promised land to my grey, rainy, cold-ass military dorm of a hometown. Twenty years later, the aura remained, with some distance, and a world of difference. The new cool called Portland, Oregon home: so said all and especially the IFC show "Portlandia," then at its peak. *Saturday Night Live*'s Fred Armisen and Sleater-Kinney's Carrie Brownstein had started in the mid-aughts a collaboration as ThunderAnt, filming short comedic sketches about endearingly and/or obnoxiously eccentric figures inspired by real life figures of the Oregon city. The slick TV upgrade of their concept was by 2014 its own phenomenon, both reflection, observation, and send-off of a scene it also contributed to popularizing.

In some ways, it was an American response to "Nathan Barley," the short-lived BBC show focusing on the London equivalent of a new youth subculture which the zeitgeist, some-how, could only name with a sixty-year-old term: hipsters.

Fuzzy as its defining characteristics were, they were plenty recognizable: a taste for obscure and edgy art and fashion, an approach to life apt to turn all choices—whether they be personal, social, political or consumerist—into fashion accessories of sorts. Nothing about this was especially new per se; but this was a subculture for the global internet age, leading a quest for authenticity and originality aiming at universal relevance, which the wider world derided as insincere, commonplace and terminally pedestrian.

It was funny to think of and funny to watch. I, of course, was not one of *them*, whether they were from Portland or any other place. The hipster is always someone else, and I, like everyone else, always knew better. I had taste but no condescension; I was worldly without being haughty; I did not value flash over substance. A bit of honesty reveals now and ever what "Nathan Barley" had illustrated in devastatingly hilarious fashion. The show's title character was the reigning king of a new wave of fashion-conscious and generally unconscious "idiots" skewered as such in the opening episode by Dan Ashcroft, a moody, down-and-out journalist forced to work for *Vice* doppelganger magazine *Sugar Ape*. But each episode shows how futile Ashcroft's knowing distance and clear-eyed analytical sense prove in the face of the cultural juggernaut he—and through him, all of us who "know better"—has to deal with. Every time Ashcroft thinks he's exposed Barley and his peers as the brainless cretins he knows them to be, they slink out of his grip, flip the script, and show Ashcroft himself as one of theirs: unwitting preacher-man to their church, pioneer to their embarrassing fashion, and follower of their most asinine trends. There is no insulting the perpetual ironist who flaunts idiocy as a form of rebellion. Worse yet, there is no outside hipsterdom: we all live in it, whether we want to or not.

That was ten years before I even set foot in Portland. And Portland was delightful. On the surface, what I saw of the Rose City was what I always wished for any place I've ever lived: a vibrant cultural life, a conscious city where cars stop for pedestrians, children are welcome everywhere, and seemingly no one would bat an eye at a quirk of any kind. The friends and acquaintances I rejoined or met there had plenty of opportunities to do the things they had once done well on the East Coast: poetry, art, music, teaching, all in various combinations. Expectedly, this kind of peace came with certain and visible ease: what I saw of the place (and granted I only got to see so much, of course) and the people in it felt casually well off, just so. Beautiful people doing beautiful things everywhere. Then and now, I figured: if this place is good enough for Consolidated's Adam Sherburne, it's fine by me.

Still, I'd be lying if something about it did not feel peculiar. It took me a minute to really put my finger on it. Not long before I was set to fly back, my friend took me to a "very

Portland" event: Swift Watch at the Chapman Elementary School, whose chimney has for a few decades been a roost for these migrating birds. Throughout the month of September, locals gather on the grass slope next to the school to watch the birds fly about. Check it out, it's on YouTube, like everything else. You've seen those flocks of swifts used as an omen in brooding HBO series and creepy movies, their shapeshifting mass a clue that something equally as disturbing as their eerily harmonious flock looms on the horizon. Yeah, I should have expected some kind of enlightenment; still, the epiphany sort of took me by surprise.

All in all, it was a fairly wholesome piece of fun. Children and some adults slid down the hillock on pieces of cardboard, waiting for the light to fade enough for the birds to get bold and start their aerial ballet. The wait gave me plenty of time to observe my fellow birdwatchers, a crowd of locals, I assumed, looking much like the audience at an Alt-J concert: tattooed, fit, casually but smartly dressed, sun-kissed, cool and *white*. So white, in fact, that it occurred to me I might be the only non-white person there. And the wait gave me plenty of time to reflect. There was no hostility; no one bothered me, stared or anything, and, mind you, I'd been to, or lived in, hegemonically though never exclusively white American spaces before: rural Illinois, Penn State, Greenwich, CT streets on a Thursday afternoon, a Murphy's Law concert. But I had come to Portland naively thinking that such a big city would feature more diversity just, I don't know, out of respect for itself. The days before, in other circumstances (on campus, at the market), the odd brown face had perhaps fooled me. But here I was on a Sunday night like the proverbial fly in the ointment. A fluke maybe, I thought on my way home.

Still, it bothered me. "Why is Portland so fucking white?" I asked myself, and as I knew next to nothing about Oregon history (didn't play that trail game either; I didn't grow up here, OK), I went the way of twenty-first-century sleuths: I typed that shit in a search engine and went in deep. And boy, did I get more answers than I'd bargained for. Fade to archival research scene.

The entire state of Oregon, it turns out, is overwhelmingly white by design: between US independence and the 1840s, both the British and the Americans had fur-trading outposts in the area and claimed joint control over it, without asking or telling the Native population with whom they were interacting. Soon they did not have to anyway: successive malaria outbreaks in the 1830s decimated the Chinook and Kalapuya living near white settlements. That decade saw a drastic increase in American population—quite a few of them Methodist missionaries, thirsty for Native souls to save. Part of the salvation package included organizing white settlers into a local government, and among the first decisions they took was to draft laws prohibiting slavery in the territory and prohibiting Black people as well. Subsequently, a series of laws would further qualify how little Black people were welcome in Oregon: a reminder, for those who might need reminding, that racial discrimination was often as strong in the Jim Crow North as it was in the South. The solution to the American "race problem" attempted in Oregon was to build an American white ethnostate—on paper, that is. None of this prevented enslavers and enslaved from coming to the territory, mind you; it just allowed authorities to pretend they were not there. As it turns out, Oregon authorities loosely enforced their hostile antiBlack laws. But then, they did not actively punish enslavers among settlers either: the ban was not on the practice of slavery so much as it was on the presence of Black people, but until the Civil War, Oregon Territory authorities would not enforce laws banning slavery either.

These exclusion laws and others specifically targeting Asians stayed in the books well into the twentieth century, and undoubtedly contributed to Oregon's utter whiteness—as did the love locals bore to such friendly organizations as the Ku Klux Klan. When the racist terrorist group found new life between the two World Wars, it took Oregon by storm: in 1923, of the two million members nationwide, 35,000 lived in Oregon (out of about 830,000 state residents). The near-complete absence of African Americans in the state did not stop the Kozmikal Dragons: there were plenty of Asian Americans and Catholics to harass, and they did so legally and in full view, as for a few years the KKK became the foremost political force in the state. Plagued by corruption and scandal (didn't see that one coming), the pillowcase scouts gradually got less cocky about parading in public in the 1930s, though one can imagine they did not actually go anywhere. One can also imagine how well they took to seeing the influx of African American people brought into the state to work in the logging industry and the naval yards as part of a plan to bolster the war effort.

Between 1940 and 1944, the Black population in Portland grew tenfold, and kept growing steadily after that until the end of the war. It did not stop the city from actively practicing segregationist redlining, but it did bring jazz to the Rose City: after major floods in 1948 devastated Vanport, where most of the Black population was settled, those who stayed relocated to the neighborhood of Albina. Portland's "Little Harlem" soon became a destination for jazz musicians, and between the 1940s and 1950s boasted a robust club scene, with Black venues like the Dude Ranch, McClendon's Rhythm Room, Paul's Paradise, or the whites-only Desert Room welcoming the likes of Louis Armstrong, Dizzy Gillespie, Billie Holiday, and local favorite Warren Bracken. In the late 1950s, urban planning took a toll on Albina and its cultural life, leaving the club scene in tatters.

There, as in Chicago and other major urban communities, when the time came to decide where new highways would be built, the easy answer was in the Black neighborhood. Authorities chose to plow through Albina and residents were forced to relocate in no time, moving into neighborhoods until then occupied by white working-class communities. Portland's Black population, redlined into a circumscribed neighborhood and subpar lodgings, constantly confronted the bald-faced racism of the Jim Crow North. Still, the Civil Rights and Black Power movements reached the Pacific Northwest. Tellingly, the most violent collective clashes Portland saw at the time occurred in circumstances involving the police and militant Black groups increasingly active in Albina. The 1967 cultural festival "Sunday in the Park" in Irving Park in the heart of Albina was set to feature Eldridge Cleaver and a Black arts theater troupe. The events started peaceably but not without tension: police presence at the event was as heavy as it had been on the streets of Albina throughout that summer. When the scheduled guests all failed to appear, violent clashes broke out between the cops and people in attendance that spilled into the neighborhood and resumed two days in a row, seeing some businesses burned and dozens of people arrested.

Two years later, Kent Ford, member of the Albina Black activist group National Committee to Combat Fascism— soon to become the local branch of the Black Panther Party— and others intervened when the police attempted to arrest a young Black boy, and tension escalated into a full-on fight. For a few days afterwards, the provocative and brutal tactics of the police incited more clashes. Several businesses burned down and mass arrests followed. The police notably targeted Ford and other Portland radical Black activists, an effort that in turn fanned the flames of discontent. Of course, the FBI's targeting of Black militant groups and active efforts at undermining them by all means available were on display throughout the country—they were all the more shocking in an area with such a small Black community, and against a group whose most visible activity was to organize a free breakfast program and free healthcare services for the Albina population. Acquitted of charges of rioting in a subsequent trial, Ford sued the police in turn and was awarded damages for the violence he'd experienced at their hands.

As in many other northern cities, in the 1970s the fight for civil rights crystallized around busing, as Albina residents opposed a plan whose solution to educational inequalities was to transport African American students out to white suburban schools. The acrimonious struggle lasted until the early 1980s. Following a massive school boycott campaign organized by

Black parents, new board of education members abandoned the policy, opened news schools in Albina, hired Black teachers and developed new curricula. 1980s Albina looked like urban Black neighborhoods the country around: plagued by slum-lord absenteeism and ignored by the municipality, until a slow trickle of white residents pushed the municipality to make the area welcoming to these good clients. Albina faced the fate of many a working-class urban neighborhood, as its location gradually made desirable a neighborhood once shunned by white residents. Since the turn of the century, gentrification has pushed a majority of Black Portlanders out of the histori-cally working-class and Black neighborhoods of Albina, Boise, Eliot, Alberta, and into the eastern ridges of the city, as their old digs became a hub for luxury condos and hip bars.

Portland's deserved reputation as a haven of radical pol-itics and living was built in the past forty years, in no small part at the expense of Black neighborhoods and culture. The cycle of economic and political violence levied at Black Oregonians follows familiar patterns, and these patterns leave their imprint on the hipster phenomenon, when they are not shaped by it: thus the insalubrious, expensive urban dwellings in which urban Black populations have traditionally been segregated are systematically "discovered" by white artistic types looking for cheap rent, a vanguard generally followed by attendant businesses—art galleries and stores, performance venues—which in turn attract bars and eateries and draw broader, hip crowds. When white numbers justify the interest of the authorities, a traditional chain of real estate schemes, increased policing and urban renewal clicks into place, until new circumstances make it impossible for the old residents to remain in place. In this way, hipsters are both symptoms and engines of racial discrimination, in Portland, in Brooklyn, in urban centers throughout the country and abroad, in culture, in economics, in politics. Yet if these cycles are not novel, they accelerated significantly in the twenty-first century.

Not by chance did "Columbusing" appear in the mid-2010s: the term, in the way it describes "the art of discovering something that isn't new" with a reference to the godfather of Native American genocide that is 50 percent snark, 50 percent historical awareness, couldn't be more hip. In this sense, it is as accurate as it is self-reflexive. Columbusing was hipsters recognizing in their typical tongue-in-cheek, ain't-I-so-clever way that hipsterdom is colonization.

So let's see where that insight takes us.

Chapter 1

LOOK AT THAT FUCKING HIPSTER

You are not what you own.

—Fugazi, "Merchandise."[1]

Look at that fucking hipster. Pants are tight, sneakers vintage and pristine; the Poison t-shirt is ironic (or IS IT?), visible tattoos are edgy, a fine trucker hat covers his tousled undercut, all manners of hair bedeck a pallid face framed by thick horn-rimmed glasses. John Brown might have approved of his facial hair, had he lived on instead of getting himself hanged fighting against slavery a hundred and fifty years ago. Loser, amirite? Ambling down the sidewalk, skinnycino™ in hand, weaving in and out of traffic on his fixie, what have you, he's on his way to his local, a former dive bar bought out by Wall Street investors and renamed *Dive Bar*, cans of PBR served in a bucket, microbrews on tap, avocado toast on the menu, you know the deal. It's right around every corner of every city now, and that is where that fucking hipster is always going. There he may meet his mates and there may well be women too—you'll know them by the fashion, the twenty different kinds of bangs, flower tattoos creeping down bare arms and mix-and-match stratas of once and future cool fashion—vintage anything, because all that is past, whether it was cool then or lame then, is cool now, all carefully crafted carelessness. You know their night

1   Fugazi, "Merchandise." *Repeater*, Dischord Records, 1990.

will be brighter than your day, Instagrammed and hash-tagged for good measure. You may only live once: hipsters live again, and again, and again.

A cliché, you say?

Of course. And like all clichés, the hipster has become part of the décor, a nuisance from the past woven so seamlessly into the fabric of our days that we no longer notice. There's no telling a hipster from a douchebag these days—both are everywhere, seeking uniqueness in universally recognizable ways. It wasn't always like this, not really. Once upon a time, in the 1990s of yore, the hipster's natural habitat consisted of specific, delimited urban ecosystems: Manhattan's Lower East Side; Brooklyn's Williamsburg; Berlin's Kreuzberg; London's Shoreditch (or the fictional Hosegate of *Nathan Barley*); Paris's Marais (aptly, French for "swamp"). Since then, hipsters have multiplied exponentially and expanded their domain. The whole world is their oyster bar now, and we all eat in it.

Yet before he was cut into pieces and scattered Osiris-like into the zeitgeist, the hipster had to be born. Though none would claim him, he had many parents, some of whom we will observe in following chapters. For now, let us just say that he materialized in the late 1990s from the same heady brew that gave us the major subcultures of the twentieth century: avant-garde art meets popular culture at some uncharted crossroads and, around innovators in art, fashion, journalism, organizing, forms a scene of connoisseurs, fans, and followers that grows as the niche goes from well-kept to open secret. But for all that a trend may owe to popular art, popularity necessarily kills its claim to artistry. A trend too popular becomes a standard, a commonplace: it finds its spot on the wall next to taxidermized narwhals and LCD Soundsystem record sleeves. It may manage to retain a measure of surprise, but once its conventions are known, it becomes part of the cultural fabric. So, arguably, went the twenty-first century hipster: he waxed (vinyl's the best), he waned, or maybe he diffused, all the more loathed because his idiosyncrasies melted in the mainstream.

Reproduction of daguerreotype attributed to Martin M. Lawrence (1808–1859). Salt print, three quarter length portrait of John Brown. Courtesy Library of Congress Prints and Photographs Division.

And so these are the 2020s, and you can no longer *really* see the hipster. He is dead, buried in 2004 and again the following year, and every year after that until about 2016, when we suddenly found ourselves dealing with much more important matters, like the death of truth. Donald Trump as president: so much for irony. But perhaps the rise and fall of hipsterdom and the reawakening of the white-supremacist beast that ushered Trump into the White House are not completely unrelated. Let us now return to John Brown, the leader of the 1859 antislavery raid on Harper's Ferry. Bear with me, or more specifically, *beard* with him and the lush wonder of facial hair he sported in his guerrilla years, a fashion statement that tripled as a religious and political statement—as Sean Trainor has demonstrated in his research, the history of American facial hair trends is political, and therefore racial. Reflecting on Brown's execution after the failed raid in his poem "The Portent," Herman Melville dubbed the man's beard "the meteor of the war." The beard stuck out from the hood which Brown was forced to wear when he was hanged, and appeared to Melville as an omen, the celestial sign announcing the upcoming Civil War. My turn then, and there she blows: from the vantage point of 2020, let me declare here (and discuss later) the hipster's undercut/beard combo a portent of its own, announcing the arrival of the orange love child of Andrew Johnson and Jefferson Davis at the White House. In order to get there, and then rampage through American streets, in full view of all, unashamed and unimpeded, the beast had to feed and grow strong. The hipster provided it with comfort and nourishment; it also offered fair-trade, Chemex-brewed cover so that the beast could sneak by undeterred and undetected. When the hipster finally fell, struck by one final opinion column, fascism rose from that empty shell, *Dreamcatcher*-style.

So that's the hipster. And you'll get there with me, eventually, but for now let's backtrack a bit. Let me sit down and, like everyone before me, ponder the indefinability of the hipster phenomenon even as I go about attempting to define it.

The common agreement is that the most recent incarnation of the hipster came about in the late 1990s. The decade boasted a few new subcultures and musical genres, easily reduced in collective memory to the sonic and visual markers they flaunted as so many anthems or flags flapping in the wind: dripping superfuzz, hunger dunger dang singing, plaid shirts and jean shorts for grunge, glow sticks and phat pantz for the candy raver, specific brands for specific scenes, so on and so forth. But the hipsters, to the extent that you saw them in relation to music in particular and culture in general, weren't necessarily attached to a particular scene so much as they boasted all-around scene savvy. It bears mentioning that the slow rise of the hipster was contiguous with the rise of indie rock, this amorphous blob of a genre label best defined in the song "Gimme Indie Rock" by one of its flag-bearers, Lou Barlow, as the latest white appropriation of the blues.[2]

An aside: Lou Barlow's short historical survey and celebration of "indie rock" was also very much a mockery of it and its heroes, even as Lou Barlow himself was well on his way towards becoming one of them. Somewhere in the potent brew of self-consciousness, self-assessment and self-deprecation that yielded Sebadoh's little gem also lurked the monster to come. Barlow knew well the utter whiteness of his being, the unspoken quest for cool that underlay all pop scenes and how, at some increasingly inchoate ideological level, these impulses both welcomed and clashed with the possibility of commercial success. But in this, he himself echoed awareness shown not by a white boy, but by Sonic Youth's bassist Kim Gordon.

On her way to becoming the eternal sunshine of the woman hipster, Gordon too had to learn. In 1989, at a time when her fame was relatively confidential but her countercultural bona fides were already stellar, she was asked to interview new hip hop sensation LL Cool J for *SPIN*. Meeting

2   Sebadoh, "Gimme Indie Rock." *Gimme Indie Rock!*, Homestead Records, 1991.

Cool James and his dance crew (including Rosie Perez) at a downtown studio, self-defined "Lower East Side scum rocker" Gordon felt "really, really uncool" and possibly a bit shocked at provocative dance moves Gordon found "more sinister than sexual," an ironic commentary on America's hypersexualization.[3] The collision of the "two sex bombs" crassly announced in the article's headline was a dud, interviewer and interviewee never managing to truly talk to each other. Doin' it and doin' it, as LL Cool J would say. They didn't do it so well, but no matter: Gordon found some hip flesh for her article, building up from the failed exchange to a tongue-in-cheek exploration of the chasm between her brand of white female punk ediginess and J's hip-hop Black masculinity.

The real tour de force occurred a bit later, when Gordon distilled the encounter into Sonic Youth's 1990 single "Kool Thing." A classic example of the band at its height, blending pop structure, punk gall and avant-garde dissonance, the song looks back in its lyrics at Gordon looking at LL Cool J, all at once mocking his earnest, spectacular masculinity, with Gordon's own laughable liberal eagerness and the peculiar fragrance of racist and sexist cliché wafting from their exchange. The video directed by Tamra

3   Kim Gordon, "Meaty Beaty Big and Bouncy." SPIN 5.6 (September 1989), 50.

Davis dotted the i's for those who could not hear, alternating between shots of the band playing in a papier mâché décor and a black-and-white fantasy featuring Gordon and a LL Cool J stand-in. Pouty Kim, dreamily petting a black cat (a nod to the cover of LL Cool J's *Walking with the Panther*), daydreams about a nameless, objectified Black man (he is the "Kool Thing" of the title, and throughout the video is often reduced to body parts—face, eyes, mouth, torso— by extreme close-ups). She unlaces his high tops with her teeth, kneeling at his feet to caress his legs. The flag-bearer of eighties political rap, Public Enemy's Chuck D, now standing in for Cool James' voice, interjects buzzwords seemingly at random. As if replaying a dialogue from one of nineties arthouse favorite Hal Hartley's movies, both voices seems to speak past, rather than to, each other. In hindsight, "Kool Thing" remains an impressive feat of alchemy, with Gordon managing to transmute her leaden exchange with LL Cool J into a golden nugget of self-deprecation and critique of commercialism. It is also eminently uncomfortable to watch, which is arguably part of the point, and makes the video a grandmother of hip irony. As it happened, "Kool Thing" was Sonic Youth's second single on their first album with a major record label: a new era was about to begin.

One last Gordon story, from the Year of Our Lord 2001. Then living in Paris (overrated), I was about to hop on the train back to my hometown in the eastern marches when I was treated to a vision of horror: gigantic posters hanging from the rafters of the train station, sporting actors and musicians posing solemnly for the camera, among them Kim Gordon—by then Queen Mother of hipsterdom—and Tricky. Those were ads for The Gap, which had just recently opened stores in London and Paris. I knew next to nothing of the brand until that moment, and its collection of bland pants and preppy tops left me thoroughly unimpressed: in fact, the only interesting thing about these clothes seemed to be the people wearing them. In order to get some name recognition in old Europe, The Gap had decided on bolstering this subtle ad campaign with free prestige concerts in both cities. The Gap Hi Fi Global Concert Tour, as it apparently was called, would feature an intriguing lineup: Tricky, Sonic Youth, Jim O'Rourke, Ikue Mori, DJ Olive, The Incredible Moses Leroy, players of fairly demanding music sitting on a sliding scale of mainstream clout—even the best known in the group, arguably Tricky, was not quite a household name—packing enough name recognition to attract numbers, and enough edginess to make this a desirable event for the in-crowd. And that—playing cool—was so clearly the point, that to a person who knew and appreciated these artists' music, the whole thing was offensive. The event was free, BUT: tickets would be given out, first come first served, at the goddamn Gap store. To get the magical piece of paper, one had to physically enter that den of capitalist depravity.

Well, reader, it might be saying something about my righteous young self that I was of two minds about this. This was before Facebook, you understand; it wasn't yet part of daily life to use seemingly free stuff meant to extract pieces of your soul for the benefit of gigantic multinational companies. This felt like a dirty trick, turning tables on music fans and move them from pontificating about artists "selling (themselves) out." No; this was about artists selling out their fanbase. I'm not sure what I thought was going to happen if I set foot inside a store I would have otherwise never even walked by. And that, right there, was the issue: I hated that I had been made to look at commodities I had no interest in, simply because of the clever use of people I appreciated for their music. I didn't like seeing these musicians' aura, which clearly affected me, attached to random crap.

All of this may seem risible in 2020, when so many artists seem to first appear to us already sponsored, if simply by the platforms out of which they rise, fully formed, like capitalistic Athenas. But so-called "affinity marketing," wherein a company partners with people or organizations with a devoted fanbase to attract them to their product, was still relatively new to me, in any case at this level of brazenness. Little did I know that using recognizable songs and musicians was one of The Gap's signature advertising moves. The company had spent the previous few years developing commercials counterbalancing the absolute blandness of their clothes with exuberant choreographies evoking classic musicals, or clever covers of famous and widely appreciated songs, or artists, actors, and musicians prancing cute around a monochrome backdrop. Needless to say, neither Tricky nor Kim Gordon nor Jim O'Rourke ever featured in TV ads: their edginess was magazine, Euro material. It was all so transparent and crass as to feel personally insulting. Early in the 1990s, Ian MacKaye of Fugazi asked in "Merchandise," a boiling, post-punk anthem to conscious anti-consumerism: "What could a businessman ever want more than to have us sucking in his store?" Not sure. But there I was, teetering on the edge of a commercial teat.

I never had to decide whether to act righteous or to line up outside a Gap store. On the eve of the day when he and Sonic Youth were supposed to fly out from New York to Paris, Chicago transplant and future fifth band member Jim O'Rourke was sitting in a studio on Murray Street in Manhattan when he heard an explosion down the street. A plane had just flown into the World Trade Center and definitively ended the twentieth century. Suddenly we were all Americans. The concert never took place.

Let's not leave The Gap just yet. It is not the worst place to sit and ponder about the term hipster, a word that was cool before the word cool was cool. That was a long time ago, though, so long ago in fact that to use it to describe current people is, well, a bit uncool. As we'll see in the following chapter, the original, mid-century hipsters were African American bebop aficionados, knowledgeable about the new, wild, and disorienting groundbreaking music, wearing garish, outsized clothes and speaking a mix of African American vernacular and insider lingo. The term eventually attached to those white people imitating Black people, patronizing the same clubs, mimicking their poses and clothing and attitudes. But it also attached to the timeline of bebop's rise and ingestion into the mainstream, stretching roughly from the early 1940s to the mid-1950s, after which hipsters themselves dissolved into beatniks and so on. So why exhume sixty-year-old slang? We all know nothing good comes out of raising the dead.

Allow me to do my own bit of quotational necromancy with everybody's favorite Karl Marx bit: "All great world-historic facts and personages appear twice . . . the first time as tragedy, the second time as farce."[4] Marx aimed this sick burn at French would-be dictator Louis-Napoleon

---

4   Karl Marx, *The Eighteenth Brumaire of Louis Bonaparte*, 1852.

Bonaparte, whose 1851 coup and self-rebranding as Napoleon III seemed to the well-bearded German philosopher an obvious and pathetic attempt at repeating Uncle Napoleon's own 1799 takeover. The use of the term hipster in the 1990s suggested that, in the eyes of the name-caller, its targets were to their 1950s forebears as Napoleon the Small was to his uncle: an homage dribbling more or less unwittingly into parody, a try so hard it deserved ridicule. Skewered in their search for uniqueness as mere repetition, neo-hipsters were not just bound to follow the way of all fashions; they were already in the dustbin of history, where they'd picked most of their articles of clothing—ironically—and like Nappo Number Three, would one day be remembered mostly for facial hairstyle shocking in its bold dedication to the grotesque (yes: that goatee extends from below the bottom lip).

And maybe that's all it was: some wicked, pointed snark. But this is the twenty-first century: we all know that we must question the observer. What do we call the hipster spotter? Mirror, mirror, who's the hippest of them all? The ability not just to spot the fucking hipster, but to point him out and mock him bespeaks an unspoken sense that our discernment is better than that of the target of our scorn. It is also quite clearly an anxious attempt at exorcising the possibility that we ourselves might have fallen victim to worse lures than the ones we describe.

First time as tragedy, second time as farce: but what becomes of farce when irony lies dead in a Williamsburg gutter, waiting to be picked up and resold at prohibitive price at the lifestyle boutique around the corner, where the kosher deli used to be? Some time in the 1990s, something peculiar happened. I remember to this day a friend of mine trying to convince my father to sell him an old Adidas track suit top. My father was horrified: he'd owned that old brown thing long enough for it to become his official gardening outfit, and could not fathom why anyone would want it, much less pay for it. I couldn't explain it either, unmoved as I was by the seductive power of ochre. The friend was dead serious, though, and his request spoke of a rising trend that would soon see luxury thrift stores sprout up all over the place—what had once been the province of the poor and the strapped-for-cash bohemian was increasingly turning into a cool thing, the clothing equivalent of the DJ's never-ending hunt for unknown vinyl (check that tech out on YouTube, kids). He'd spotted a specimen in the wild and was hoping to snatch it before others sniffed it. Another portent: soon, cool-hunting would be the order of the day.

Considering why the word "hipster" was exhumed in the late 1990s to characterize this new breed of cultural Nimrods, Mark Greif proposes that at that moment, "their look was still continuous with the short-lived neo-Beat one 50s nostalgic hip moment . . . the earliest new hipsters may have looked enough like the old hipsters of dim mid-century memory to call up the name."[5] Blame it on the thrift store, but also on a peculiarly constant state of revolving cultural nostalgia, the advent of what Simon Reynolds dubbed "the 'Re' Decade." The neo-beat moment followed in the footsteps of a neo-swing moment that saw young Americans dressing like old Americans and learning acrobatic steps their grandparents might have practiced—if they were cool, that is. I don't need to tell you what clothing brand used all this to sell khakis. I'll tell you anyway: of course it was The Gap, who also tapped into country line dancing, sixties go-go dancing, *West Side Story*, Depeche Mode. The store even summoned Bill Withers for a "khaki soul" commercial displaying more dark-skinned people than usual, in unusually grey tones, because why the fuck not? Real cool people have Black friends.

The Gap's conjuring of increasingly close past cool music to impart cool on their current clothes is a quintessential example of how "retromania"—the frantic, accelerated version of cultural nostalgia Simon Reynolds diagnosed—has become the principal cultural dynamic of the digital age. In this light, the term hipster itself appears all

5   Mark Greif, "Epitaph for the White Hipster," *What Was the Hipster?: A Sociological Investigation*. Mark Greif, Kathleen Ross, Dayna Tortorici eds. (New York: n+1 Foundation, 2010), 141.

the more inadequate and pedantic that retromania typically follows a much narrower cycle centered on "fashion, fads, sounds and stars that occurred within living memory."[6] You might have been tickled that the riff of The Strokes' 2001 single "Last Nite" was shamelessly lifted from Tom Petty's 1976 hit "American Girl." Petty himself took it with good humor. The video for the song, the work of Roman Coppola, might as well have been shot by his father Francis in his youth, say between *The Godfather Part II* and *Apocalypse Now*, so much did the video's set, the footage's grain, and the band members' style look as seventies as the song and musicians they ripped off in the first place. More unsettling yet was that this commitment to retro was an essential part of the band's cool, as if unabashedly Led Zeppelining "American Girl"—a favorite of oldies stations throughout the country and hardly a groundbreaking track in the first place—should somehow be seen as innovative. You could pretend to edginess by spit-shining dull old cafeteria knives and claiming they were blades.

In the nineties admen were already on it, and they found an increasing number of consumers ready to let brands help them believe they could somehow eat their consumerism and have their edginess too. The whole thing seemed simultaneously flippant and earnest, models hovering between

6   Simon Reynolds, *Retromania: Pop Culture's Addiction to Its Own Past* (New York: Farrar, Strauss and Giroux, 2011), xiv.

1000-watt cheeky smiles and pouty, Zoolander-like affected seriousness. What authenticity was claimed here lay all in self-consciousness as a pose, real or itself fake, on and on in an endless loop. Whether you liked Depeche Mode or not, The Gap's a cappella version worked either as homage or parody: it was reference-for-reference's sake, an orgy of post-modernist, self-conscious games of citation devised to hide that getting access to, and potentially possessing everything—for a price, of course—did not in fact provide more meaning to our lives. In this field of ruins strewn with pieces of what we thought were monuments of culture, the market remained as the last structure standing, impervious to witty sarcasm.

Back to that godforsaken Gap concert: in the usual cycle, edgy artists would gain popularity on their own terms before seeing their novelty gradually caught up with and swallowed by the mainstream, changing said mainstream a bit in the process, maybe. But here, the mainstream declared, in a shocking reversal, that these artists were always already part of us. We *knew* too. We get cool. And this reversal made resistance seem not only futile but worthy of mockery, snobbish, so that the very distancing at play in calling someone a "hipster" reverted upon itself. Who the fuck did I think I was, thinking my tastes were so much ahead of everyone else's, thinking I could obtain and listen to the music others made for a living and somehow eschew capitalism and commercialism?

History, worldliness and irony suggest there is no escaping the system, in the end, so what else to do but join, enjoy and laugh, as bitterly as you want? There's a niche for that too. The former tenets of subcultural scenes—independence, a more or less tacit code and related behavior—all these dreams of integrity could be derided as naïveté: what of these used to relatively protect scenes, if not make them hermetic, was made moot by the internet and the new understandings of belonging it developed. The internet did not make access equal, but it increased it, and gave it a pretense of globalism.

But as always, some people are more global than others; where the DIY spirit of punk rock and hip hop could be a way of life and a politics, as a global commodity it became increasingly one option among others, one of many dishes in a cultural smorgasbord. With cool now easily and increasingly available, connoisseurship became more than ever a matter of access and consumption rather than participation. As Greif put it, hipster today identifies "a subculture of people who are already dominant. The hipster . . . aligns himself *both* with rebel subculture *and* with the dominant class, and opens up a poisonous conduit between the two."[7] That conduit turned the quest for cool—once registered as non-conformist, even when undertaken safely and comfortably by upper-class

---

7   Mark Greif, "Introduction," *What Was the Hipster?*, 9.

individuals—into just another commodity. As it turns out, this one could be bought equally well with economic, cultural, or racial capital.

Belonging to a subculture or a niche used to demand some sort of commitment, paying some dues: one could dress and act punk, certainly, but anyone who's ever opened an issue of *Maximum Rock 'n' Roll* knows that the scene engaged in near-constant conversations about authenticity—who was a poseur or a sellout—and that these conversations pointed to anxieties of belonging entirely alien to the modern hipster. Hipster 2.0, the discerning, all-encompassing individual consumer, thinks of himself as a curator of sorts, whose informed and tasteful choices make into a subculture of one, however much he ends up looking like the hipster next to him. He "understands consumer purchases . . . to be *a form of art*."[8] This quest for uniqueness and taste led, among other things, to initially ironic reclamations of the erstwhile uncool—and few things until then had been so profoundly uncool to the white American middle class as the white American working class and poor. Hipsters 2.0 traded the fetishization of Blackness of their predecessors for that of the "violence, instinctiveness and rebelliousness of lower middle class suburban or country

8   Greif, "Introduction," 12.

whites."[9] Hipsters may well admire, hang out with, or even accept in their ranks non-white people—they exist, I have seen them—but hipsters are overwhelmingly—enacting self-awareness and contentedly so, at that—white.

There is nothing new in the well-off appropriating working-class stylings: "nostalgie de la boue," that attraction for "low" culture, as we will see, is as old as fashion perhaps, certainly as dandyism. The difference here, arguably, is all in the intensity and the racial self-awareness that accompanied it. The cliché signifiers of white working-class subculture—the trucker hat, the handlebar moustache, redneck tattoos and Midwestern and Southern motif t-shirts—that became typical of hipsters were worn precisely for the utter whiteness they represented, the irony resting necessarily on the very menace these signs packed.

In turn, what edge one might have found in the specificities of female hip were often layers of fresh paint covering the unique angles of working-class queerness with conventionally gendered provocations. Oh look! It's Bettie Page again. The paint contained more irony than lead; what of punk dejection and riot grrlishness it inherited, mixed in with precise or smeared makeup, only reinforced hipsterdom's endorsement of a basement porn visual aesthetic that

9   Ibid., 10.

no sarcasm could redeem. Much of the visual style of the women of hipsterdom as it circulated in magazines and online depended on the calculated outmodedness of the Polaroid: a testament to their unspoken commitment to overexposed whiteness. It also looked up to the sulky sublime embodied by Chloe Sevigny or Rosario Dawson since their debut in Larry Clark's *Kids*, arguably a harbinger of the most extreme aspects of this aesthetics. Hipsters manifested "not as a subculture but like an *ethnicity* . . . coded 'suburban white,'" notably in their endorsement of styles and fashions generally marked as unsophisticated and derivative by connoisseurs of cool.[10]

Indeed, much like Gap commercials, the references themselves often read as a peculiarly bleached rereading of history. If original hipsters pillaged their name, along with the music, style, dance, and attitudes of Black artists and audiences, hipsters 2.0 could afford to act as if Black people had never had any import, if they so chose: it worked as irony or as provocation. Consider Marty McFly, thrown back in time, nonchalantly rewriting history by introducing Chuck Berry to his own "Johnny B. Goode"—think of this gross travesty, repeated as a farce that would be all surface. A testimony to the broad reach of the hip plague, that pattern was echoed by artists themselves. Jack White and the Black Keys started a

10   Greif, "Epitaph," 147.

feud over which pale-ass guitar hero served the best regurgitation of sixties pale-ass white kids' regurgitation of rhythm and blues—and that made the cover of the *Rolling Stone*. White told the venerable magazine, in all seriousness: "I'll hear TV commercials where the music's ripping off sounds of mine, to the point I think it's me. Half the time, it's the Black Keys," going on to explain what differentiates his brand of retromania from the Black Keys' in shamelessly commercial terms: "certain acts open up a market for a certain style."[11] Way to open up a market, Jacko. Latter-day hipsters and their icons could just pretend they did not need blackness at all, notably by imitating the original white imitators, and presenting that imitation as innovation.

Pastiche more than parody, then: Hipster 2.0 perfected his grandfather's technique with the fancy new tools at his disposition. Let's see how we got here in the first place.

---

11   "Jack White: The Strange World of a Rock & Roll Willy Wonka." *Rolling Stone*, June 5, 2014.

Chapter 2

FROM THE HIP

"There is nothing wrong with material possessions. But you should use them and not let them use you. I think everybody wants to conform, but the future of the world lies in the hands of the nonconformists. . . ."

—Ted Joans[12]

The original, mid-century hipsters were African American bebop aficionados, knowledgeable about the new, wild and disorienting groundbreaking music, wearing garish, outsized clothes and speaking a mix of African American vernacular and insider lingo. The term eventually attached to the white people imitating the Black people, patronizing the same clubs, mimicking their poses and clothing and attitudes.

Whoa. Was that déjà vu? Yes: you read this in the last chapter, but also, yes: over and over again. But it's deeper than it seems: hipsters have a history, and it's not just on a twenty-year rotation. It's not all about facial hair and duds either. "Hipness," Robin James tells us, "is a practice grounded, both historically and structurally, in racism." Worse yet: "discourses of taste and hipness produce individual bodies as white, and maintain Whiteness as a socio-political norm."[13] That's right: the history of hipsters is a not-so-secret history of race in the Atlantic world. That's why you should pardon my French:

12   In Fred W. McDarrah, Gloria S. McDarrah, Beat Generation: Glory Days in Greenwich Village (New York: Schirmer Books, 1996), 5.

13   Robin James, "In but not of, of but not in: On Taste, Hipness, and White Embodiment." *Contemporary Aesthetics* 2 (2009). http://hdl.handle.net/2027/spo.7523862.spec.209

there are of course national particularities to hipsterdom—as anyone who remembers skinny pants once being derided as "European" knows well—but they do not trump the cross-pollinating transnational, transatlantic practices of casual race-building that underlay hipstory (yeah, I went there).

Whew. Ready? So let's start with the term again, and dig.

A hep-ster, a hip-ster, a black and tan scenester, but then again, not always: if the suffix -ster denotes belonging of some sort, then this connotes a belonging to hip, or hep. At the turn of the twentieth century the term "hep" or "hip" sneaks into the American English language, of origin officially unknown. Unknown, that's never stopped anyone from speculating, or tracing genealogies of usage, as one does. And so there are interesting etymological lines out there.

That is what dictionaries say, but were we to wade a little further upstream, we might ponder the relation hep or hip might have to "hip hip": before this became the cheer to which all would respond "hurrah" sometime in the late eighteenth century, "hip hip" was an interjection, what you might say to hail someone in the street or, if you were a shepherd, to your sheep as you lead them to their pen or, if you were French, to the waiter who's been ignoring your gesticulations for the past half hour (hint: hailing is not the way to go) or, if you were an early nineteenth century German anti-Semite, to your fellow bigots as you rampage through the streets of Würzburg or Frankfurt assaulting Jews and burning down their houses during the 1819 "Hep Hep" riots. No one really knows why the rioters used the chant that came to name this infamy, but a longstanding, popular conspiracy theory assigns it a sort of secret meaning as a rallying cry supposedly passed on to nineteenth-century anti-Semites from crusader anti-Semites. The truth of the story matters less than what it highlights in the usages of hep/hip as a call for recognition that expects a response, whether those you call for are strangers on the street or fellow racists.

What could this possibly have to do with hipsters? I'll tell ya. Cultural appropriation wasn't born in a day, or in twenty-first-century Brooklyn: rather, contemporary hipsters are the latest variation on an age-old cultural tradition. The central elements of hip—clothes, attitude, music, insider knowledge—lead to the history of Atlantic slavery and to the central fact that modern culture as we know it owes a whole lot to the African diaspora.

For centuries, millions of Africans were captured to be sold into slavery in the Americas and be worked to death and abused, their labor, their bodies, stolen from them. The many slave societies that developed in the Americas had their own specificities inflected by the cultures of the colonized, American and African, and those of the colonizers from all over Europe. They were all similar in that with time they built legal, social, economic and proto-scientific systems of racial discrimination meant to justify and perpetuate themselves. Laws regulated how the enslaved should work, where they could go, but also how they should be: where and how they might congregate, what language they should speak, what food they could grow, eat, sell, what musical instruments they could play, what dances they could dance, what clothes they could wear. From South America to the United States by way of the Caribbean, increasingly elaborate laws banned the playing of drums or dancing in public; from the early 1700s on, laws in the Caribbean and Louisiana specified what Black people could wear, and forbade Black women to show their hair and risk outshining white women.

The first laws to discriminate against all Black people, irrespective of their free or enslaved status, listed the specific fabrics they were allowed to wear. In order to build race, enslavers felt they had to also control fashion. Not that it worked as planned: there were always ways to follow the letter of the law and challenge it. Even as enslavers would do the bare minimum to provide clothes for the enslaved and restrict what they could procure for themselves, the latter still managed to develop unique styles and fashions from, and against, the material restrictions imposed on them. Black women turned the tignon—the headdress they were forced to wear—into an art and a secret language. They subverted the law by following it to the letter, using colorful fabric to design elaborate headdresses; in Martinique, for example, the manner of folding the madras headdress communicated information about the wearer's love interests. Similarly, if the enslaved wore the same drab clothing in the fields, on weekends and holidays they went all out, affecting what colorful clothing they could obtain at dances and celebrations. In the face of systemic oppression, dehumanization and enforced humiliation, messing with dress codes, subtly appropriating and reorienting material elements meant to visually represent control was a form of sub rosa resistance and imperceptible commentary, clear enough to those in the know, and dissembling enough not to warrant systematic punishment.

Enslavers tolerated this sartorial defiance, not necessarily aware that there, as in the United States, the extravagant dress and dances often subtly mocked enslavers. More importantly yet, as Shane and Graham White contend, the fashion sense of the enslaved was "an emphatic repudiation of their allotted social role" that "intruded . . . into the world of their supposed betters."[14] Such laws were meant to create and enforce racial separation and difference in domains of life where they were dangerously tenuous: it turned out that

14   Shane White, Graham White, *Stylin': African American Expressive Culture, from its Beginnings to the Zoot Suit.* (Ithaca: Cornell University Press, 1998), 35.

no matter how dedicated to discrimination white people might be, they nevertheless still found the arts of people of Africa appealing and wanted to appropriate them. Black cuisine, clothing style, music, and speech infused American white cultures, and just as quickly they traveled freely across the Atlantic. European fashion flowed into the American colonies, but colonial fashions sailed back as well, bearing unmistakable traces of the Black Caribbean styles born of coercion in the late eighteenth century.

The so-called "Creole style" of dress, for example, featured white, diaphanous dresses made of muslin, a fabric traditionally used for women's underwear in Europe and generally considered a logical answer to the torrid climate of the tropics. Just as often, Creole style included variations on the headdresses Black women were forced to wear, but whose sophistication and class became the envy of white women. The Creole style of dress made its way to Europe and took off there in the dying days of the Ancien Régime, only to be adapted later into the neoclassical style made popular by the likes of Madame de Récamier, Thérésa Tallien and other prominent women of the new French ruling class, most notably Joséphine de Beauharnais and her friend Fortunée Hamelin, both heiresses to wealthy families respectively from the French Caribbean colonies of Martinique and Saint-Domingue.

In the aftermath of the Terror, moderates took control of the French Republic, organizing a new government, the Directory. As they were drafting a new constitution, fearing that the Jacobins who still had plenty of popular support might try to regain power, the moderates allowed the sons of the upper middle-class to organize in roving bands to harass radical Jacobins on sight in the streets of Paris. These cane-wielding goons were known as "muscadins," after the strong perfume they were known to douse themselves in. They made sure that their ideological differences did not just smell but also showed: you could tell them by their extravagant, spilling neckerchiefs and tight, garish coats. With the Jacobins under control, the new rulers of France cracked down on muscadin street gangs, but their ideas and fashion style remained.

Their successors, the "Incroyables," affected a peculiar, possibly English-inspired accent—dropping "Rs" supposedly because the letter reminded them of the hated revolution—and further amped up clothing outlandishness, wearing their undersized riding coats unbuttoned, or bunched up so as to mimic a hunchback, their hair short on the neck and drooping long on the sides, like dog ears. They might wear a single gold loop earring, known in France as a "creole." Like their close relatives, the British dandies, the Incroyables cultivated expertise in the trivial and claimed fashion discernment as their paramount quality, which they demonstrated, not without humor, by perpetually carrying quizzing glasses, with which to inspect whatever or whoever might need to be. Yet perhaps even more than the Incroyables, it was the most famous among their female counterparts—the Merveilleuses—who embodied Directory France's aura of glamour, sex, and scandal mostly attached to women and their fashions.

Newspapers throughout Europe regaled their readers with anecdotes about the lusty ladies of the Directory, their scandalous dugs, their libertine behavior, and shameless love for that provocative new dance out of Austria, the waltz. They delighted in describing with great detail the increasingly more risqué outfits—all transparent materials with next to nothing underneath—women introduced at the many parties they attended, but also, sometimes, in the streets. On one occasion, as she was stepping out of a carriage on the Champs Elysées in one of her signature tulle dresses, slit on the side all the way to her hip, arms bare and cleavage showing, Fortunée Hamelin, accompanied by an anonymous friend, found herself harassed by passers-by who soon gathered into a crowd and forced the women to flee the scene. Though all the fashionable women of the Directory adopted these new, sulfurous styles, few were so admired and stigmatized for it as Hamelin.

FULL DRESS

PARISIAN LADIES in their WINTER DRESS for 1800

"Parisian Ladies in their Full Winter Dress for 1800", an over-the-top exagger-ated satirical Nov. 24th 1799 caricature print by Isaac Cruikshank, on the excesses of the late-1790s Parisian high Greek look, and the too-diaphanous styles allegedly sometimes worn there.

Clichés about the lascivious nature of Creoles in the torrid zones were already part of popular culture, but rumors according to which Hamelin's mother might have been a free Black woman only exacerbated the deluge of lustful comments about her. Even as Hamelin's reputation grew too scandalous for Napoleon's new regime, her salon became Paris' most fashionable social circle, where Europe's prominent artists and politicians routinely gathered. For the best of the following four decades, Hamelin remained a central figure of France's highest social and political sphere. In case you were wondering what slut-shaming was like during the Enlightenment, Hamelin remains known as "the naughtiest person in France," the nickname she earned in her days as the queen of Merveilleuses.

The Directory initiated a familiar pattern: European fashion tapped into fantasized and fetishized notions of Black-infused exoticism, only to deny that they influenced anything at all. In this way, Hamelin's own life reads like a running metaphor: after Bonaparte overthrew the Directory and got himself named France's First Consul, he had Hamelin (who had once been his lover and forever remained his loyal confidante) banned from the court, as he strove to impose a façade of respectable behavior. A year later, Bonaparte would send a massive expedition to the colonies in order to reestablish slavery, simultaneously closing continental French borders to Black people. No matter: Black cultural influence always finds a way. The Black insurgent army in Saint Domingue defeated the French and declared independence on January 1, 1804, becoming the first free nation in the world. North of Haiti, in the United States now expanded by a third after Napoleon dumped Louisiana on rapist-in-chief Thomas Jefferson, Black people had to cope with surviving in the first white supremacist Republic in the world.

As the free Black population grew in North America and throughout the Caribbean, despite increasing legal segregation so did cultural exchanges. Northern whites kept African Americans in distinct neighborhoods which they often had to share with poor whites. Faced with constant abuse and extreme racist violence, African Americans also found themselves the objects of intense and obsessive scrutiny. White fascination with Black style fed a stream of ethnographic accounts simultaneously marveling, ridiculing and expressing anxiety at the sight of the Black "dandies and dandizettes" who were strutting their stuff in urban centers throughout the Americas. Whites hated it, but also couldn't get enough: Creole songs and Caribbean-themed plays were all the rage in European capitals in the eighteenth century already, where actors such as Charles Mathews made their reputation rendering "true" interpretations of Black Americans, their speech, their singing, their dancing. Imagine a male Iggy Azalea in breeches and actual blackface, telling London crowds he's the realest. Throughout the cities of the Eastern seaboard, white performers, songwriters, and writers mocked and emulated Black festivals, celebrations and balls. By the time American entertainer T. D. Rice figured he could stomp around New York stages in blackface doing his own impressions of Black speech and dance as a character he named Jim Crow, the ingredients in this cake recipe had been around a while. Look at the cake, copy it, slap some icing on it (make it Black), sell it as the real thing: you're a baker now.

And so blackface minstrelsy took the country by storm, and also Great Britain, and on through Europe. Let's say it again for the kids in the back: the pattern of fascination, scorn and shameless pilfering that structures minstrelsy is the basis on which American popular culture rose, and I don't mean just the United States: Rice echoed Mathews and eighteenth century English comedies set in the Caribbean; plays featuring Creole songs and dances were performed on French stages, and Caribbean basin sounds and style were all the rage in nineteenth-century France as well, where half a century before jazz was even a thing, New Orleans composer Louis Moreau Gottschalk moved to make a living coating Black music he'd heard growing up in European frosting. This was late-1840s Paris, and the art scene belonged to the bohemian. Ancestor to the hipster if there ever was one, the bohemian

was an idle young man who chose eccentricity over con-
formity and art over convention. Whether or not he actually
did make art as the bourgeois might understand, the bohemian turned anything he did into art. That could be writing,
sure, painting, why not, making music, possibly, but it could
just as well be talking shit, dressing fancy, or acting cool.
Bohemians' scorn for, and dedicated opposition to, the pillars
of bourgeois society—family, work, virtue, good taste, common sense—their cult of pleasure, art, frivolity set standards
of behavior that underlie to this day what we expect of artists
and hangers-on.

You may not be surprised to find out that at a time when
Black presence in Paris was fairly minimal, Black people were
disproportionately represented among the bearded ranks of
la Bohème. France was developing its own peculiar rapport
to American Blackness and its own brand of erasure as well:
though the bohémien is part of France's cultural clout in
and outside the country, there is virtually nothing left of the
Caribbean bohemians in popular memory. If poet Charles
Baudelaire is the first name to come up when you think
of these circles, you may then also know of "Black Venus"
Jeanne Duval, the Caribbean actress who was his partner
and muse for many turbulent years, but chances are that you
know her by the slanderous, condescending, sexist accounts
reserved for her by generations of Baudelaire scholars—a

racially ambiguous slut-muse in the lineage of Hamelin. Most French people have never heard of the likes of the Caribbean Eugène Chapus, Melvil-Bloncourt or the Louisianian Victor Séjour, stalwarts of the scene.

Yet it so happens that according to all parties involved, the quintessential bohémien was a free Black man from Guadeloupe by the name of Alexandre Privat d'Anglemont. His friends and acquaintances undeniably admired him, his dandyish style, his nonchalant attitude and impeccable wit—but they just as clearly saw these wonderfully decadent aspects as intrinsically related to his blackness. Anglemont was the absolute bohemian, the bohemian naturalized, because his exoticism made him an outsider, the perfect challenger to French bourgeois values in that his opposition literally showed on his skin. White bohemians, then, had in him a model to emulate that they could never quite attain. The pattern set by bohemians was that of praising a vision of the noble savage as one to emulate and perfect. Paradoxically, Anglemont was celebrated for his dedication to art and artifice—style—in the same movement that these qualities were presented as natural to him. By this token, then, the mere fact that this behavior supposedly did not come naturally to white bohemians, their having to work at it, made them more sophisticated bohemians.

Maybe this kind of praise made Anglemont snicker: most of what we know of him is secondhand, conveyed by friends and acquaintances who, as much as they liked him, seemingly never found out for sure how much of what he told them was made up or real. At least they had some notion that Anglemont was talking shit. But then, he was also talking shit without having to fear the repercussions the enslaved would have had to face on the island where he was born, or in any other slave society in the Americas. Those who had to talk shit more subtly developed, for instance, the cakewalk: a dance birthed in the mid-nineteenth-century US by the enslaved, it parodied the stilted ballroom dances enslavers were fond of. Said enslavers found these shenanigans so entertaining they took to awarding cakes to the best dancers—hence the name. Taste the irony and consider the existential meaning of "being hip" in circumstances where smarts and wit could end your life. This tradition and art of creative irony you may know in many different forms as signifyin': saying one thing in the language of the oppressor while meaning another.

Enslavers regularly unleashed brutality for much less than mockery: why risk so much for so little as momentary, secret satisfaction? I don't pretend to understand it fully, but then I also think we all get it: the power in small acts of agency is how we keep going, how we nourish our souls. Poking fun at enslavers in these ways, the enslaved literally ate their cake (the one they won at the dance, remember) and might have it again the following week, with a little more flash, a little more bounce and, more importantly, while making sure the knowledge remained secret enough to at least keep enslavers guessing. To be hep, if the word had existed then, might have meant to be in on the joke, aware that it even was one, when enslavers looking down on them thought they had it all figured out. All groups of the African diaspora around the Americas developed similar small acts of cultural sabotage, and ways for obfuscating them, allowing irony to pass for simple-mindedness, and yet coding it all in secret languages and signs accessible only to what future NAACP secretary James Weldon Johnson would call the "freemasonry of the race": those who know, enslaved or not and soon no longer really enslaved, but still subjected to the same blanket oppression and continuing to make ever-changing lemonade from an endless deluge of lemons. Black American cool thus rests in no small part on the communal knowledge that this life in the heart of whiteness is a dangerous game with ever-changing rules. Signifyin' can be seen as a series of calls and responses, check-ins of sorts, hailings, where every subtle joke or nod asks someone else: Get it? Hip?

Hip.

But being hip can't forever remain a sort of secret knowledge; this affected hermeticism, otherness claimed, boasted

A "Cake-walk" dance number from the musical comedy Florodora, *performed in Stockholm, Sweden in 1903. Courtesy Wikimedia Commons.*

and blasted could only attract outsiders, whether they be actual enslavers, or white people of all walks of life and even, possibly, a modicum of sympathy for Black people. For every Anglemont, there was a white man to explain him, the original cool peeled and reconstructed by immediate witnesses to the broader circles of the white public. The same pattern obtained at a broader level, leading to regular cycles of mainstreaming of Black culture. Here's a quick summary for your enlightenment: the cakewalk craze at the tail end of the nineteenth century sailed in the wake of minstrel shows and ushered in ragtime, and soon enough jazz, rooted in the blues, all-Black musical genres in a segregated society that magically turned American as they took over the entire world and changed global popular music.

France became jazz's home away from home: during World War I, African American soldiers had been treated halfway decently by the French and some, like bandleader Jim Europe, came back, carrying in their suitcases the new music and inspiring many other Black artists to follow. Among jazz's earliest supporters were notably avant-garde artists, many of whom owed at least part of their sulfurous reputation to their shocking admiration for the arts of African people, in the visual arts, sculpture, music. Cubist painter Fernand Léger was instrumental in putting together la Revue Nègre, an all-Black cabaret spectacle performed by a troupe of African American musicians and dancers including an unknown eighteen-year-old woman named Josephine Baker. She featured in a suggestive, exoticizing "Danse Sauvage" with Réunion-born French dancer Joe Alex, American and French Blackness united on stage expressly for white spectators' ogling pleasure. The drooling testimonies of fascinated reviewers contributed to making Baker and Alex overnight sensations. The Revue opened the door to American jazz, but also to Caribbean music. Martinican clarinetists Alexandre Stellio or Sam Castendet had their day in Paris as France's sudden love for all things Black also got metropolitans suddenly interested in the music of the old colonies. They truly began the beguine by bringing it to Paris, where they mixed the Caribbean genre with jazz before it picked up American shores.

Jazz quickly became an international phenomenon, developing at the crossroads of American, French and Caribbean culture and unique brands of racism and fetishism. White Frenchmen's fantasies and delusions about Black life in the Americas fed into the jazz craze in Paris, but it also informed white American outlooks: the desperately white authors of the so-called Lost Generation, contemporary with those of the Harlem Renaissance, had relatively little interaction with them in the US. But in Paris, Hemingway and his pals hung out at African American queen of the night Ada "Bricktop" Smith's cabaret; Gertrude Stein and Alice B. Toklas's circle (Djuna Barnes, Janet Flanner, Solita Solano) lived queer and free-love and reported back to the US on the follies of Parisian nights. The coolest of them all was the Englishwoman and Modernist icon Nancy Cunard, a poet, journalist, translator and fashionista, sponsor and muse to artists and fashion designers. The violent reactions she experienced due to her relationship with African American pianist Henry Crowder beginning in the late 1920s contributed to her awakening to racism, and eventually to her editing and publishing the *Negro Anthology* in 1934, a monumental documentary volume showcasing the arts and cultures of the African diaspora. Cunard remains an anomaly in how little she benefitted personally from closeness to Black culture. The figureheads of the Lost Generation, one foot in Gay Paree and the other in American publications, made proximity into sheen for their cool, modeling a sophisticated and safe form of engagement with Black popular culture crucial in the genealogy of hip.

In France, African American performers were openly admired and respected for their craft, a contrast drastic enough with the situation in the US to cement France as a haven in the African American cultural imaginary. Those who knew—say, veterans—knew. They were hip to it, although by then, hip might refer to something altogether different.

The infamous Eighteenth Amendment of 1919 banned the production, sale and possession of alcohol throughout the United States, forcing a thirsty nation to learn how to imbibe subtly. You might find speakeasies, blind tigers or blind pigs, or take your booze to go, in which case you would need a discreet vessel for your hooch. Say a hip flask. Carrying one of those would make you a hipster, an urban cowboy taking shots from the hip, if you will.

The state of drink also made France all the more appealing, certainly. Back home, white hipsters might well drink their booze somewhat discreetly in jazz clubs, but drinking was no longer so legally comfortable. Not to mention the little matter of the country's racist brutality: the late 1910s saw the Ku Klux Klan come back with a vengeance, the organization growing to record numbers, and not just in the South. The time period also saw a spate of citywide assaults on African American people culminating in the infamous Red Summer of 1919, which saw mobs of white people rampaging through Black neighborhoods killing hundreds from Washington, D.C. to Chicago, Baltimore to Omaha. In 1921, a rabid mob razed Greenwood, the Black section of Tulsa, Oklahoma, massacring hundreds of people and displacing thousands without generating as much as a single conviction. When they did not massacre Black people, white Americans in all corners of the country practiced various forms of segregation.

Jazz clubs such as New York City's famous Cotton Club were not spared: they generally banned Black patrons (or otherwise had segregated nights), though they might use exclusively Black staff and the Black entertainment stars of the day. Even when the shining stars of jazz were recognized, it was to the extent that jazz was being digested and regurgitated by white America. Consider this: the great Duke Ellington may have been broadly considered musical nobility in the 1930s, but the so-called "King of Jazz" was a bandleader whose idea of bettering jazz was to cut down on improvisation, a white man by the name of . . . Paul Whiteman. You can't make this shit up.

Prohibition was repelled in 1933 but the term hipster remained, possibly maintaining some of its risqué overtones in sliding from hooch to hoochie coochie, black bottom, Charleston, jitterbug, you name it: the acrobatic dances of the swing era held sway over ballrooms, Black or not. "Nordics," as poet Langston Hughes called them, did not want Black people in their clubs, but they were not above slumming it uptown to observe the new dance steps formulated in Harlem dance halls, Now that everybody was drinking steadily, hipsters no longer needed flasks: their very hips held the truth and they brought the hurt to the dancefloor. The term was used for all genders to emphasize the sexual overtones of jazz dances: before Elvis the Pelvis, there were hipsters, male and female agents of dance contamination. These were hipsters and there were hepsters, those in the know, again: they knew how to dance, they knew how to dress, they knew how to act, how to walk the walk and talk the talk. Denizen of the jazz scene, connoisseur of cool, the "hep cat"—as defined by the great swing vocalist, "Hi De Ho Man" Cab Calloway in his *Hepsters Dictionary* (1938)—"a guy who knows all the answers, understands jive." Through swing, the vocabulary of African American jazz musicians passed to the circles of fans and hangers on that formed the immediate scene around them—a specialty language the understanding of which delineated who was in and who was out. Being hip, then, again, was to know what others—outsiders to the scene, squares—did not. Not until they bought the dictionary, in any case. Hip hip hurrah.

But by 1938, jazz and swing were not only mainstream American music, they were what the world thought of when the world thought of American music. Calloway's dictionary was welcome, I'm sure, but then it was a sure sign that Black cool was going through another round of digestion. Swing was the music, hep cats wore outsized zoot suits and matching outsized hats which, though they met the usual mix of scorn and awe from the wider white society, were already widely imitated by the start of World War II. Double-entendres and signifyin' remained, but the music industry was well in control of a music now tailored to sell and repeat over and over again what sold. What small victories—individual or collective— had once occurred between two trumpet solos were likely of little comfort, as Black entertainers saw the benefits of their music fall to others. White musicians, sure, bandleaders and other stars, but even more the music industry, whose captains were in the business of scamming all talent, notably by withholding all royalties from records sales from musicians. The record companies' greed led to a massive recording strike of the powerful American Federation of Musicians: between 1942 and 1944, professional musicians and members of the union could perform in concerts but not in studio recordings. Neither could they hold jam sessions, an activity for which the union could and would fine them.

A rare haven in these peculiar times was Minton's Playhouse in Harlem, a club run by Black union delegate Henry Minton where down-and-out musicians could always find food and shelter, but also where the jam ban did not apply. Minton's was a safe haven and what transpired there, as Black musicians hanging out afterhours found themselves free to experiment away from the public's expectations, fundamentally revolutionized the music. The story goes that Charlie Parker, Dizzy Gillespie, Thelonious Monk, Miles Davis, et al. wanted a music that white musicians could not play—they set out to make just that, deconstructing swing into bebop in small committee while the innocent majority kept dancing to the same old tunes. The ban on recording kept the new music a kind of secret, known only to a happy few. You know where this is going: around the inner circle of avant-garde musicians were other musicians fascinated by the new sound, if not necessarily able to play it, and then little by little, those listeners who "got it": cool kids only at first and for quite a while, until the end of the strike and the end of the war allowed bebop to take American eardrums by storm.

But first bebop shocked precisely those it was meant to shock: those who could not play, who did not understand what it was doing, or how. There's a case to be made for the irony woven into the genre. Covers have long been a feature of popular music, but what bebop did to preexisting songs and compositions was something different altogether: it took them and undid them, mocked them, celebrated them, cited them to build upon them. A sonic cake walk. Bebop was complex and clever and it drew strong lines between those who got it and those who did not. Early on, those lines were as segregated as anything else in the US—but the power dynamics were drastically flipped. Not an unfamiliar pattern you'll say, and you'll be right (thanks for paying attention)—arguably, the African American musical tradition is also a tradition of entertainers finding new ways to tell their white audiences to kiss their Black asses (see Amiri Baraka's *Dutchman*). But here was music you could not quite dance to, and musicians who did not seem to want you to dance; here were entertainers who seemingly dared you to like music that upended everything you thought you knew. A challenge for you to get hip. You already know how that went.

For our purposes though, we should linger on precisely those people, the non-musicians who got with it. The first fans of bebop were Black people who, like Langston Hughes, recognized in the music's name an echo to police batons cracking Black skulls. They shared with their forebears a full awareness of American racism; the change, according to the ethnographers that came out of the woodwork, was apparently in the existentialist flavor they brought to it. Not a random term here either. French existentialism very much translated as a scene, in the US. Paris as Americans had found it after four years of German occupation had turned a bit darker but still packed a titillating punch: Saint-Germain des Prés, cigarette-smoking, black-clad brooding bohemians hanging out in dungeons listening to jazz. It was beat before beat was a thing, and it gave African American musicians and writers a welcome akin to a homecoming: Richard Wright and James Baldwin made a home there and then, Charlie Parker, Dizzy Gillespie had Boris Vian and Jean-Paul Sartre as guides, Miles Davis and Juliette Greco fell in love. The French way, then as after

WWI, relied on treating Black artists decently, recognizing their talent, and seeing being where white America saw nothingness. Part of the history of hip is transatlantic ping-pong, and this was round two.

Anatole Broyard's 1948 "Portrait of a Hipster" posited that the essence of hipsterdom entails a dramatic quest for recognition in a society designed to deny Black existence. In the article, which was already a postmortem, Broyard argued that the bebop scene's growing popularity tolled the end of the Black hipster experiment—interest from white intellectual circles and the following recognition, paradoxically, did not fulfill the quest but shone a light on its utter irrelevance, and placed the hipster alongside his forebears in the diorama of American subcultures. Then as now, much of the reflection of critics over hip was a reflection over critique. Pinning hip, naming it, taxonomizing it meant erasing the secret knowledge and therefore the very essence of hip, and this was what he saw in the circles of dejected whites now dragging themselves out of jazz clubs and through Negro streets at dawn, as Allen Ginsberg would howl, and whom no one called a beat just yet. There is no small irony in the fact that Broyard had a secret of his own: he passed for white throughout his life. But this secret element, arguably, points both to the same old dynamics of appropriation: what the pillagers of hip described by Broyard were desperately looking for, again and always, was Blackness. And they could not get it.

But they got plenty out of it: by the late 1950s, beats and hipsters were the latest fad, rejected by and rejecting Eisenhower's America, bearded and be-sandaled denizens of Greenwich Village where they spent days doing nothing and nights reading poetry in smoky coffeeshops. A little bit of Saint-Germain on the fringes of Eisenhower's America: way to spice up that cake. Hipsters were hip and they were worrisome because their taste of bohemia carried with it a bit of danger. They lived in a working-class-adjacent neighborhood and you could go visit them there, a form of slumming that was comfortably white, all the way around. Endless op-eds and articles on hipsters followed, until the epitome of them all: Norman Mailer's 1957 essay in *Dissent* "The White Negro: Superficial Reflections on the Hipster." There's much to lament about Mailer's bloated prose (it's almost as long as two chapters of this book, come on!), starting with its bile-summoning title, but let's mention how Mailer fairly accurately identifies "the Negro" as "the source of Hip," only to explain how driven by "the art of the primitive, he lived in the enormous present, he subsisted for his Saturday night kicks, relinquishing the pleasures of the mind for the more obligatory pleasures of the body." Mailer's back to the hips: in his mind, it's all about first-person liberation from the fetters of society, i.e. it's all about killing and fucking. Alrighty then.

For much of his essay, Mailer did what many had done before him: he marveled at the magic of Black people. But perhaps more importantly for the rest of our timeline here, he argued innovatively that hipsterdom was rooted in a form of envy for a fanciful idea of Blackness (which Mailer himself apparently thought was real). The piece itself, arguably, was evidence more than demonstration, and Mailer, in his classic ethnographer's stance, very much part of the issue he pretended to analyze. Picking up where Broyard had left off, Mailer saw the hipster as an American existentialist hero (forget the French), presenting in the process Black people as a natural resource of sorts. Not cake: pearls, sitting quietly at the bottom of the ocean waiting to be plucked out of the depths by knowledgeable divers who might then mount them for necklaces or whatever it is you do with pearls. Plenty of eyes rolled at Mailer, but it fell to Herbert Gold to point to the blinding whiteness of his reflection. "A colored hipster, by this definition, is a Negro Negro," said Gold, nonsense unmitigated by the fact that Mailer knew plenty of Black hipsters himself.[15] But Mailer's argument took for natural law

15   Herbert Gold, "How to Tell the Beatniks from the Hipsters" (1960). In Fred W. McDarrah, Kerouac and Friends: A Beat Generation Album. (New York; William Morrow, 1985), 166.

a system of cultural and commercial exploitation, and figured he could dive deep enough into the American psyche to
observe all the divers, not noticing that he was himself so full
of wind that he would come bobbing up to the surface, again
and again to see nothing but his own white face, superficially
reflected there, on the waves his essay made.

For all the critical distance with which Herbert Gold
looked onto "White Negro," he nevertheless rode on its
waves too, at a time when Mailer's hipster had given way to
the beatnik, who was "the hipster parodied and packaged as a
commercial product . . . a commodity" that is to the hipster
"as the cornflake . . . to a field of corn."[16] And so here we
were, as the commentators of yore were writing obituaries
for hipster forebears: standing on the shoulders of Black folk
and paradoxically pretending that merely recognizing Black
contribution was enough to justify erasing them. Over and
over again.

It's not going to get better.

16   Ibid., 167.

Chapter 3

HIPSTER FASCISM

"From the beginning of time, the bad guys always had the best uniforms. . . . I mean, the SS uniform is fucking brilliant! They were the rock stars of that time. What you're gonna do? They just look good."

—Lemmy Kilmister, *The Guardian* 7 January 2008

Hey, guys, how about a fashy? Not you, girls. Hitler hairdos aren't cool on the ladies. Trust me. But get that hairdo, guys. Or don't. Whatever you want to call it—high and tight, undercut, Hitler Jugend, fashy—its coolness has come and gone: when everyone has had it, you know it's over. Or do you, though? Hair is trifling, of course, of course. But as an outward sign, a proclamation, as the way fashions and subcultures present themselves to the outside, it matters. The undercut is the outward expression of a subculture that in the moment wants majority clout with the trappings of minority status. In this sense, it is whiteness personified. The latest return of the hipster was accompanied by a higher dose of racial self-consciousness—and not necessarily for the better. The twenty-first-century hipster ushered in the age of Trump and unabashed, self-aware white efforts at inner colonization. Just like in the olden times, but with a hefty veneer of irony, just in case he might have to deny it all at some point.

The first time I heard Radiohead's "Karma Police" was when their third album *OK Computer* first came out, because I'm not a child and I've been alive a while. We listened at a fun party in an unfamiliar house, but mostly I remember the general mirth and how drastically it contrasted with the casually sinister sense of foreboding radiated by the album. And it played, in its entirety, over and again. But this isn't about the music so much as the girl in the song's lyrics—the one in the Hitler hairdo, who makes the list of potential targets for the Karma police. Something about the cut gives the song's speaker the pukes. Fair enough.

Hitler's slicked down hair strand/Charlie Chaplin moustache combo is a trademark recognizable even in the absence of a face, or slapped onto someone else's. Cool women of the 1990s went with slicker takes on the fearful asymmetries of the punk era, but this particular one wasn't such a common 'do for women or men in 1997, except in certain circles, and arguably, calling it a Hitler hairdo was not meant as a good thing: whatever the singer has against this poor girl, he's out to piss all over her stylistic choices. Because he could have called it something else, really. Barbers do.

The popularity of the undercut owes the Austrian pig nothing: most agree that it appeared in the late Victorian era and was favored by English working class and street toughs: it was a neat and stylish signature look, and some suggest the same reasons made it popular among soldiers in WW1 and in its aftermath. By the 1930s it was everywhere, including on the empty skulls of Nazis from Hitler Youth to the Gestapo. In the second half of the twentieth century, the haircut never disappeared but as long hair returned to fashion, notably in reaction against the alleged conservatism of shorn hair, the undercut came to occupy a peculiar in-between—aggressive in its sharp contrast between short and long, ambiguous in its politics. By the 2010s, like hipsters themselves, it would become ubiquitous even as all pretended it to be elusive. While hip women happily pick their hairstyles from decades of cool, reintroducing Rosie-the-Riveter-style updos, demonstrating the unsung versatility of bangs, experimenting with the irony of perms and dye or not, male hipsters flocked to the fashy like sheep to the shearer. But until the twenty-first century you might see the likes of it in circles where it's OK to shave the sides of your head AND have the rest long enough to cover your eyes—namely, the subcultures of the skinhead/punk nebula. And in the cultural and political analysis of haircuts, inches have long been imbued with disproportionate meaning. Now, now.

In this effort at meaning, in the late 1960s the skinheads made a very drastic commentary: shaving one's head and dressing in working class respectability at the height of flower power was a fashion statement—although hardly the hip thing to do in 1969, certainly—if ever there was one. It should come as no surprise by now that even skinhead fashion, related to Mod fashion as it was, at least as far as clothing and musical tastes were concerned, also borrowed ostensibly from Jamaican *rude boy* fashion. Mods expressed their rejection of hippie style and politics by committing to a form of working-class chic: shaved heads, neatly pressed buttoned down and polo shirts, suspenders, rolled jeans and work boots. The ladies sported similar styles, sometimes swapping short skirts and mary janes for the same boots/jeans/polo combo as the boys. They wore their hair short and feathered, developing by the turn of the 1970s a distinct 'do: the Chelsea Girl, featuring close-cropped hair on the skull with bangs down to the eyebrows in the front and worn long in the back as well: a mutant mullet from Hell. Skinheads also listened to, and played their own versions of, the Jamaican-born musical styles attached to *rude boy* culture: rock steady and ska. Drawing on transatlantic mythologies of working-class toughs in express contrast with the peace and love offerings of hippie fashion and its descendants, skinheads also reveled in violence: against hippies, against South Asians, against rockers. The first skinhead wave did not last: by 1972 it had all but disappeared, tasted, chewed up and spit out by the rising glam rock and pub rock scenes.

Skinheads did not catch on in the US then, but the country had its own related developments: in the early 1970s, rock critics Dave Marsh and Lester Bangs first started using the term "punk rock" in reference to unadulterated, raw and brash garage rock and its immediate descendants, notably the New York Dolls and Detroit's Stooges and MC5. Not unlike

UK skinheads, American punk rock was reacting against the affected sunniness of latter-day hippie music and style and the bloat of prog rock. Punk rock bloomed at the confluence of popular music and radical art, and its pioneers soon found a capital in New York City. Andy Warhol's early protégés The Velvet Underground, Patti Smith, the New York Dolls, Television, the Ramones, the Dictators, Blondie, et al. formed part of a bohemian scene of expanding influences and styles, whose stomping grounds in New York City cover an ever-Eastward progress. If beatniks had Greenwich Village, the sixties and seventies hip/art New York scene gradually moved to the East Village and Max's Kansas City (closed in 1981), the Lower East Side around CBGB's (1973-2006) with punk rock and Tribeca with the more artsy Mudd Club (closed in 1983), and eventually across the bridge into Williamsburg. Proto-punk thrived on the "seediness" of its surroundings and took advantage of its relative cheapness, yet in many ways part of its aura was to show itself as *in* it but not *of* it; adopting these local traits by aesthetic choice rather than social or ethnic nature, so to speak. The press and many performers themselves were also quick to present their music as antinomic, if not outright hostile, to contemporary commercial genres of all sorts, some of which like funk and disco were marked as Black. Part of the appeal of punk was precisely the pretense of not seeking to please, the affected scorn for appeal, however finely honed, designed and rehearsed such scorn might be. Placing the geographical heart of the scene in an area of the city considered undesirable worked well with the spirit of the scene—the Lower East Side was seen as a dangerous, lawless, savage place on the outskirts of whiteness. But in turn, the scene was the arrowhead of gentrification, and scenesters were inner-city frontiersmen of sorts, learning a bit from the natives, and effectively using this knowledge to (re)claim the grounds from them.

The MC5 notwithstanding, proto- and early punk rock was for the most part affectedly apolitical, if not antipolitical, a stance expressed in a variety of iconoclastic attitudes. Consider punk clothing: willfully jarring, featuring seemingly ill-fitting, repurposed clothes, torn fabric stitched back askew, Nazi and Soviet paraphernalia worn for shock value, spiky and asymmetrical hairdos. These provocations are usually understood to have traveled from the US to England in the luggage of Vivienne Westwood and Malcolm McLaren: before working their Situationist-inspired dark magic to mold the Sex Pistols out of thin air into the second most influential boy band ever, working on the insight that pose weighed as heavy as the music itself, Westwood and McLaren had designed the New York Dolls' outfits and public personas.

Yet the two Brit brats of fashion's totalitarian shtick weren't rock 'n' roll's first brush with fascist fascination.

David Bowie expressed his interest in Nazism and the occult throughout the 1970s, but at the onset of the punk era he went about as the Thin White Duke, a sinister, cocaine-fueled alter ego wont to sing the praises of fascist leadership and the rock 'n' roll savvy of Adolf Hitler. As often was the case, Bowie was ahead of the curve: UK punk would be replete with facile evocations. Mick Jones' pre-Clash pub rock band London SS, The Vibrators titling their song "Nazi Baby," Joy Division frontman Ian Curtis' fascination with Nazis (see the evocation of Rudolf Hess in "Warsaw" and the Hitler Youth drummer boy on the cover of *Ideal for Living*), The Sex Pistols's "Belsen Was a Gas," and Sid Vicious sporting a swastika, while hardly political creeds, were all meant to shock parents, bourgeois and the establishment alike and arguably succeeded in doing so, if only for a time.

Provocation is not innocent. No twenty-year-old growing up in the 1970s in Europe or the US could have had any doubt as to the connotations and political impressions made by swastikas, especially at a time when racial strife was boiling over in the UK. In the late 1970s, the fascists of the British National Front made significant gains in local elections and sought further national relevance, notably by taking to the streets and to football stadiums, concert halls, and any other place they might find dejected white kids to commit to their cause. Skinheads, back with a vengeance in the wake of punk, were to play a highly visible part in this. Although the late seventies revival bands (Madness, the Specials, etc.) echoed the scene's original tastes and influences, many among the newfangled skinheads also connected to Oi!, a genre in drastic contrast to ska or reggae. This specific turn away from Caribbean sounds and culture, steeped as it was in the radical dissonance of punk, was also a hard turn into whiteness. Here, what Dick Hebdige calls the "frozen dialectic between white and black cultures"[17] went subzero.

While some in the second skinhead wave were committed left wingers or socialists, a hefty plurality claimed to be "apolitical"—a suspect insistence on neutrality given the rising polarity—and a new surge of self-avowed fascist and Nazi elements delivered the movement to infamy. Outright fascist groups were on the fringe of UK politics, but in the late 1970s they gained spectacular popularity, and went looking for manpower—a pattern that would prove inspiring in later years. Racist skinheads became the street militia of the National Front and British Movement. The poster children for the embrace of fascism were undoubtedly Skrewdriver, originally an Oi! band that turned full-on Nazi in its second incarnation in the 1980s, their frontman Ian Donaldson becoming a card-carrying member of the BNF. Yet Jamaican

17   Dick Hebdige, *Subculture: The Meaning of Style* (London: Routledge, 1979), 69-70.

popular culture and music was a reference for UK punks and second wave skinheads, who found in reggae a companion and model genre steeped in political discourse. There was plenty of nihilism to go around in UK punk rock, but the genre also made it its mission to treat the problems of the day, generally with a fairly radical stance and a dose of racial awareness: think of The Clash's debut single "White Riot," whose lyrics—inspired by clashes between Black youths and the police at the 1976 Notting Hill Festival—encouraged white English youths to follow that example.

Though relations to Black culture in the US punk scene could be equally open and collaborative—arguably the most influential band in hardcore punk was Bad Brains, an all-Black D.C.-based band whose legendary concerts inspired a scene that gave us Henry Rollins, Minor Threat and Fugazi, to name but the obvious—they were also routinely fraught. The political stakes in the US could appear less urgent in the early days of punk, but similar developments soon occurred. Commenting specifically on the New York scene in 1979, Lester Bangs noted: ". . . after a while this casual, even ironic embrace of the totems of bigotry crosses over into the real poison."[18] Irony, arguably a staple of hipsterdom, allows one to eat one's cake

---

18 Lester Bangs, "The White Noise Supremacists," *Village Voice*, 30 April, 1979. < https://www.villagevoice.com/2020/01/05/the-white-noise-supremacists/ >

and forever have some left (or, arguably, right). The rebellious stance characteristic of hip and avant-garde can either translate into political action or at least discourse, or remain something short of that, snark without critique. Stay there long enough and you'll have snark for snark's sake (say that real fast many times), an outlook that demands that anything serious always be taken down a notch. Analyzing his own partaking of ironic racial slurs, Bangs argued that "another reason for getting rid of all those little verbal barbs is that no matter how you intend them, you can't say them without risking misinterpretation by some other bigoted asshole; your irony just might be his cup of hate."

And there you had it, and still do. By the early eighties only the most naïve could assert that the punk scene and its derivations could somehow pretend to be apolitical: violent racism, an inherent part of American life, was also present in punk rock. What rhetorical distance there may be between the ironic Nazi and the dissimulating one was routinely crossed as genuine Nazis showed up, welcome or not, at punk concerts. A match made in Hell, or in Orange County, California, where the KKK, Tom Metzger's White Aryan Resistance and Bob Heick's American Front started recruiting in punk ranks much like their English counterparts. When Nazi skinheads first appeared in the US, they made their home on the same sunny beaches. The Dead Kennedys' 1981 single "Nazi

Punk Fuck Off" evokes the fights that became more common as boneheads clashed with increasingly politicized, often anarchist, punks.

Punk and the post-punk scene are relevant to late 1990s hipsters as ancestral and revered scenes, and ever-ready sources for models, sincere or ironic, known or obscure. They also reveal that hipsters didn't turn Nazi overnight. Nazi and fascist imagery was spreading more or less subtly in other offshoots of punk rock. Thus New Wave—notably at its confluence with the nascent industrial/electronic scenes of the early 1980s—had quite an influence in making the aesthetics of totalitarian regimes "cool." Many New Wave bands wore matching suits and ties when they weren't going all out for uniforms. Joy Division is a notorious example, but the trend was not unique to punk rock: think of the El Lissitsky-inspired cover of Kraftwerk's 1978 album *Die Mensch-Maschine* featuring the band members in matching red shirts and black ties and slicked-back hairdos, to the clothing style, album covers and videos of pioneering industrial bands from Slovenia's Borghesia and Laibach to Belgium's Front 242. Recycling WWII-era sounds and speeches became a staple of the rising electronic genres. Here also one could argue a world exists between the shock-the-bourgeois eagerness of Foetus's "I'll Meet You in Poland Baby"—a song with cartoonish lyrics sung in the voice of Hitler to a background of air-raid sirens and German speeches—or even the chilling, tasteless paeans to serial killers, extreme violence and abuse of the likes of Whitehouse, and the fascist beliefs expressed in the musical musings of the so-called "dark folk" or Europagan music scene. But this world is a spectrum along which listeners, fans and political operators alike can travel back and forth gleefully.

"Dark folk" developed in the late 1980s at the confluence of punk, folk and industrial music, exuding fascination for occultism, paganism considered as expressions of ancestral European culture. The scene gravitates around singular figures such as the Englishman Douglas Pearce, founder and prime mover of Death in June (whose name evokes the massacre of S.A. cadre by the S.S. in the Night of Long Knives, and whose songs routinely evoke occultism and Nazism), or Frenchman Eric Konofal and his one-man act Les Joyaux de la princesse, whose every album centers on figures and events of the prewar and WWII era—notably Philippe Henriot, "the French Goebbels." Both men have been known to perform in dubious uniforms: Pearce has worn Waffen SS garb, while Konofal has sported the uniform of proto-fascist French paramilitary group Croix de Feu. As many performers wading in these murky waters do, Pearce and Konofal generally claim to be driven by historical curiosity. Similarly, Boyd Rice, arguably the most controversial figure of the experimental/industrial scene—though he infamously appeared alongside Bob Heick in an American Front uniform in the pages of *Sassy*, and as a guest on Tom Metzger's TV show *Race and Reason*—routinely claims not to hold white supremacist ideas. Just trolling, man. Don't you have a sense of humor?

Across the world, the visibility of skinheads grew, enhanced by their participation in high profile acts of violence. In Europe in particular, their presence among football hooligans made them continent-wide bogeymen as stadium violence reached ignominious peaks. The 1985 European Cup final opposing Liverpool FC to Juventus Turin at the Heysel Stadium of Brussels saw Liverpool hooligans charging Juventus Turin fans. The fray led to 39 deaths and hundreds of injuries: in the aftermath of the disaster and for a while after that, a story gained traction according to which the violence had been started by supporters of Chelsea and Leeds, English teams known for their violent skinhead factions, when Liverpool fans had ties to labor unions and left politics. This legend, whether it first came as a mistake or a lie, says something of the aura that surrounded skinheads at the time and which only grew as skinheads supporting continental teams such as Paris Saint-Germain's Boulogne Boys, the ultras of S.S. Lazio's Curva Nord or Zenit Saint Petersburg's Landscrona, to name a few, made their own reputation for racist abuse of players and violence in the stands.

The post-Heysel ban of English clubs from European competition and the 1989 Hillsborough disaster—unrelated, it turned out, to hooliganism, but blamed on hooliganism all the same by authorities eager to hide their responsibility—in which 96 fans died in a stadium stampede led English authorities to crack down on violent fans and fundamentally rearrange stadium structure and fan policing. In a decade, they effectively eradicated terrace culture and in the process forced hooligans to temper their stadium behavior—and style. The 1980s saw the rise of so-called casuals, dressed in sneakers and trainers and a variety of combinations involving elements of skinhead clothing, notably favored brands such as Lonsdale sportswear, Fred Perry polos, Ben Sherman shirts, and Doc Martens boots. By the 1990s, these same elements had all but gone mainstream.

Much could be said about the vagaries of footballers' hair fashion; before the mullet was known under that name in France, it was known as the Chris Waddle, after the English midfielder who inexplicably made that high crime against coiffure popular among French youths in the late 1980s when he played for Olympique Marseille. Yet the skinhead style and its evolution, visible as it might be among fans in the stands, rarely translated to the pitch, Paolo Di Canio being the cropped hair, sideburned, sieg-heiling exception to the rule. But at the turn of the twenty-first century, the undercut descended on football fields like a biblical plague, and it's OK to blame David Beckham, but only if we consider him as the face of several overlapping but distinct phenomena: on one hand, a level of celebrity unheard of until then. Fame has long been a global affair for football players; but the 1990s saw an unprecedented influx of money into the sport, notably by way of advertising and endorsements, these moving into individual contracts more than ever before. There had been world stars of football before him, but arguably none so image-conscious. Beckham was not the first footballer to dress up, but he took it to another level, notably as far as hair is concerned, bringing the undercut to the masses.

Let's pause here a minute.

Consider this: You'd be hard put to think of a more globally public face than Beckham at the turn of the twenty-first century; this kind of fame might seem to fly in the very face of hipsterism. Beckham himself, husband of Spice Girl fashionista Victoria, was tapped into the zeitgeist and riding the wave of fashion rather than following it, and in this way, he can be seen as a symptom of the global banalization of hip. The cyclical nature of fashion always sees the vanguard integrated into the mainstream, but the means of media circulation etc. contributed to create an unheard-of situation: at the turn of the century, the hipster phenomenon was in the paradoxical position of being a global niche. Before undercuts started blooming on soccer players' heads like poppies in Flanders fields, Beckham was a niche seen weekly by millions across the world, including, importantly, in the US, a country until then generally impervious to soccer and related fads.

To be clear: even Beckham would not have been enough to impress American audiences. But then, he was not the only one sporting it. "The Hitler Youth" or the "Jugend," as some had taken to calling it, along with elaborate, Victorian-looking facial hair, were fast becoming visual staples of the new hipsterdom. Jokes, ya know? It was ironic. And the great thing about irony, is that thriving as it does on ambiguity, it cannot possibly be coopted.

What made a strict, short undercut ideologically suspicious in the early 1990s was its existence at the confluence of trends delineated above: it was part of the ironic arsenal of the New Wave crowd. It evoked a time period more than specific political allegiances though, as we've seen, the references were to the Third Reich more often than not. Shaven skulls becoming too ostentatious at a time when many fascist parties were developing strategies to appear more respectable, the strict undercut became common among former Nazi skinheads and fascist militants trying to look approachable. Maybe it looked cool; it also looked downright sinister (Latin pun, everyone), but ordinary enough to allow doubt. A skinhead wears his identity on his cranium, and hopefully qualifying details (shoelaces, patches, tattoos, all of the above) that might allow for distant recognition: he declares himself in a sartorial combination meant to be unambiguous. The integration and repurposing of these elements into mainstream fashion brought an extra serving of doubt along with it: you might dress like a skinhead but not *be* one.

In fact, sporting a skinhead getup with an ever-so-slightly longer haircut, from buzzcut to undercut, entertained a confusion welcome by a new brand of fascist goons and operatives but also by fashion-conscious denizens looking for an edge. It should come as no surprise that many of the prominent figures of the Europagan/dark folk scene also had links to the New Right and the infamous think tank GRECE (Research and Study Group for European Civilization) of Alain de Benoist, who would come to inspire the American alt-right. In this context, the comeback of the undercut necessarily carried extra meaning. The Hitler hairdo in "Karma Police" may or may not belong to an actual fascist; she may be ironic about it, or her asymmetrical cut may be entirely the victim of undue hostility, but once seen, it cannot be unseen. Ambiguity goes both ways, and already in 1997, there was plenty of space to wonder. You know: ironically.

And this brand of irony was in the process of getting seriously monetized. Enter Gavin McInnes, in many ways the embodiment of the twenty-first-century hipster: born in

England, grown in Canada, the human moustache founded *Vice*—arguably one of the press organs most influential in integrating the new hip into the mainstream—along with Suroosh Alvi and Shane Smith in 1994 Montreal. As the story goes, *Vice* rose from punk fanzine to multimedia empire along with the newfangled hipster scene it both sprouted from and helped go global. *Vice* became known for approaching topics, serious or outlandish, with a trademark tongue-in-cheek tone, an in-your-face aesthetic and hefty servings of misogyny, homophobia, and racism—in a spirit echoing that of bourgeois-shocking avant-gardes and provocateurs for a century or two, it was eager in irony, committed to not caring as it chronicled with amusement the world—"a lad magazine for the Williamsburg set."[19] With time and success, *Vice* grew more seriousness, gaining critical acclaim for its cutting-edge reporting on difficult topics and hard-to-reach subcultures the world around. Despicable elements of the spirit that defined early *Vice* survived in its later incarnation as information colossus, as suggested by relatively recent reports on rampant sexual harassment in the organization.[20] Still,

19   Vanessa Grigoriadis, "The Edge of Hip: Vice, the Brand." *New York Times*, 28 September, 2003. https://www.nytimes.com/2003/09/28/style/ the-edge-of-hip-vice-the-brand.html.

20   Emily Steel, "At Vice, Cutting-Edge Media and Allegations of Old-School Sexual Harassment." *New York Times*, 23 December, 2017. https://

much of *Vice*'s lasting popularity rests on the more engaging elements of a spirit that helped shape the hipster moment by channeling the radical ethos of previous subcultures.

Indeed, in many ways, *Vice* applied to its era a recipe at least as old as the punk rock celebrated by the magazine's founders, as McInnes declared in a 2002 interview: "The first thing is that we all grew up with punk-rock backgrounds . . . a lot of our articles start like a punk rock song. They start heavy, and we're always concerned about the lede. And it never really slows down." Beyond these musicological musings, the interview is interesting for the genesis of McInnes, as it catches him at an early stage of his growth. Before he became the founder of the fascist gang the Proud Boys, McInnes was a loud brat dabbling in precisely the same swamp described by Bangs two decades earlier, where racial slurs are somehow edgy and cool. And so in this interview, the *Vice* edgelord just let it all hang out: "The punk rock-ness of that is just plain honesty. We seem really racist and homophobic because we hang around with fags and niggers so much. It just becomes part of our vernacular."[21] Sure, dude.

www.nytimes.com/2017/12/23/business/media/vice-sexualharassment. html.

21   Adam Heimlich, "Vice Rising: Why Corporate Media Is Sniffing the Butt of the Magazine World." *New York Press*, 1 October 2002.

This was bad enough, arguably, as was the first hint of McInnes' stomach-churning admiration for Pat Buchanan, but this is not the quote that got McInnes in hot water. When the interview was written, *Vice*—dubbed by *Rolling Stone* "the hipster's bible"—had just moved to Williamsburg—the hipster Mecca—and when the interviewer asked "Don't you get hostile being in this neighborhood every day?", McInnes responded: "Well, at least they're not fucking niggers or Puerto Ricans. At least they're white." McInnes would later go on the record claiming this had been a misunderstood joke. The evidence? A visual joke lost on those who could not see the paper version of the interview: the photo featuring the three friends had Smith and McInnes standing proudly next to a sitting, seemingly disheveled Alvi holding a handkerchief to his head. Smith was dressed like a Scottish casual, in trainers and a Partick Thistle jersey; McInnes, head shaved, arms crossed in defiance, was dressed in a skinhead-meets-*Clockwork Orange* getup, white pants and white Fred Perry polo shirt and thin suspenders. See where I'm going with this? Only a year later, McInnes infamously proclaimed his pride in being white, adding "I don't want our culture diluted. We need to close the borders now and let everyone assimilate to a Western, white, English-speaking way of life."[22] Alrighty then.

---

22   Grigoriadis, ibid.

McInnes's 2002 quote, for all the outrage it was bound to rouse, also diagnosed a peculiar development. Throughout the twentieth century, Brooklyn at large and Williamsburg in particular had been home to factories and to the working class in the image of the overlapping waves of immigrants from Europe and later the Caribbean and South America. Starting very slowly in the late 1970s, artists attracted by the possibility of renting large commercial spaces at low prices started settling in a neighborhood divided between Hasidim, Latinx, and Eastern European communities. The late 1990s saw the familiar cycle of gentrification begin, as rock venues started opening (think L Café, Stinger Club or Galapagos) and more artists and musicians moved into the neighborhood. By the turn of the twentieth century, Brooklyn in general and Williamsburg in particular had become the capital of an indie rock scene featuring such local luminaries as TV On the Radio, the Yeah Yeah Yeahs, Grizzly Bear, The National, Les Savvy Fav, or LCD Soundsystem, to name but a few in a scene musically diverse but drawn together by place, attitude and publicity by the likes of *Vice*. As always, spectators followed on the heels of creators, and by 2002 Williamsburg was the place to be for anyone claiming to know anything. The influx of hipsters and the real estate boom that always follows also spelled the end of affordable rent for historic Williamsburg communities. In short, the white hip bourgeoisie was pushing out the working class, and that is exactly what the snarky fashy McInnes was noting with glee.

Though colonization means erasure, displacement, assault, those aren't its only modes of functioning. Hipsters systematized and weaponized ostentatious celebration of the very cultures they threaten, touting their favorite mode of cultural vampirization as an identity of sorts. As he blossomed into a full-on white supremacist troll, McInnes went on the record to downplay the influence and presence of Black people in punk, specifically, demonstrating once more that hell hath no fury like a white man talking out of his ignorant ass. Lest we forsake accuracy, even in that moment of terminal whiteness, not all hipsters were white. Hipsterdom in all its incarnations has no qualms taking what it wants anywhere it finds it: because its founding logic is consumption, anything is up for grabs. We have a drastic example of this flattening of social and racial debates by way of cultural consumption in Afropunk.

Around the time McInnes was getting his supremacist jollies in Williamsburg, DJ and party promoter James Spooner was tramping the same grounds seeking out Black people he'd run into on punk stages and in punk audiences, asking them about the peculiar two-ness of being Black and Punk in America. Raised on hardcore and DIY on both the East and West coasts, Spooner had come to an all-too familiar epiphany: though punk, like all of rock, could not have existed without Black people, its mostly white members collectively could not be bothered to recognize Black punks as such, much less celebrate them. Talking about race around punks was a special kind of taboo—as an exotic, disembodied hip hop phenomenon, "Kool Thing" could only be mocked or revered at a safe and sanitary distance, it seemed. "We know you're Black, just don't tell us" says Jimi Hazel of 24-7 Spyz, describing the unspoken vibe of the scene for *Afro-Punk*, the documentary film Spooner shot between 2001 and 2003, interviewing Black musicians and scenesters alike about their experiences.[23]

Subsequently, Spooner took the film on a nationwide tour, screening it wherever interested people might be, usually as opening act to a concert or several. Warts and all, Spooner's film rallied a community. Two years later, with the help of music manager Matthew Morgan, Spooner organized the first Afropunk festival: four days of film and music screened and performed between the Brooklyn Academy of Music, CBGB's and the Delancey, featuring erstwhile little known acts such as Philadelphia punk band Stiffed with frontwoman Santi White (not yet Santigold) or a certain Janelle Monáe. The festival grew exponentially,

23   *Afro-Punk*. James Spooner, dir. 2003.

taking over Commodore Barry Park in Fort Greene to offer a yearly serving of free Black punk rock and related flavors. For a minute there, the tables did turn: here was punk celebrating Blackness.

But Afropunk had to go the way of all good things: started by misfits, for misfits, it morphed quickly and drastically. Spooner quit in 2008, but Morgan was only getting started. With attendees soon numbering in the tens of thousands, the festival expanded to include an increasingly broader variety of musical acts, a longer list of corporate sponsors, VIP passes and other Coachellaic developments. By the time it started charging an entrance fee in 2015, Afropunk was arguably one of the coolest festivals around, but not really so punk anymore; after DIY came slickness; after self-made style came fashion; after the freaks came the beautiful people. In short, Afropunk precipitated and welcomed the closest thing we may have gotten to Black hipsters, bottling up Black irreverence into a spicy product—many different levels of intensity available on location. The booths multiplied, the food trucks got fancier, editions of the festival popped up in Atlanta, London, Paris and Johannesburg, fashion magazines and people came to see and be seen.

We know you're Black: don't tell us, sell it to us. By the turn of the 2010s, Afropunk was concluding a full transformation into an Instagram-ready, glossy, prestige package putting the skater punk on display, fees keeping the gutter punk at bay while catering to the boujee up to cosplay for the weekend. The inevitable happened. As surely as a biblical plague of locusts, white people descended: tentative at first, but eventually bolder, secure in the knowledge that the festival's commercialization meant they too could simply buy themselves a sense of belonging. Let's just say that in recent editions, the sight of Biff Tannen types strutting in Birkenstocks and varicolored dashikis was hardly uncommon. Beyond the eternal philosophical dilemma of balancing out the demands of punk ethics against the finances an event of this scale necessarily demands, the gentrification of Afropunk is a perhaps unique example of a near-full circle—an event built and created by African Americans on the premise of reclaiming Black relevance from the pit of white cultural erasure, gradually distilled into a product fit for (white) hipster consumption.

Ultimately, it may well be true that "being a hipster is not compatible with being Black;" but it remains predicated with exploiting Blackness—including Black critiques of whiteness—like a bottomless mine.[24] The final stage of

---

24 Carvell Wallace, "Being a Hipster Is Not Compatible with Being Black." *Vice*. 16 December, 2015. https://www.vice.com/en/article/kwxy7x/hw-the-black-hipster-that-never-was-456.

the cultural white supremacist is to recognize and flaunt this much like his forebears flaunted colonization itself. The writing was always on the wall: it was an ironic racist graffiti done in chalk on the original red brick wall of the old bakery taken over and turned into a thrift store.

Hindsight is a few years later, after the internet, after 4chan and reddit and trolls and shitposting and Gamergate and memes, after McInnes left *Vice over* "creative differences" (*cough* FASCISM *cough*) and found his true calling as a fascist goon culminating in the 2016 electoral campaign, when he founded the Proud Boys, a twenty-first-century fraternal order avowedly dedicated to drinking beer and loving the West, no women allowed. But a silly-ass name (borrowed in typical ironic fashion from a song in *Aladdin*), and dedication not to spill their seed willy-nilly (in order to make the group's second degree of initiation, members have to forfeit porn and masturbation) are not the only values they share with this other international order of conservative boys, Baden Powell's Boy Scouts: the Proud Boys also love a uniform, and theirs—a black Fred Perry polo with yellow stripes—channels, unsurprisingly, skinhead fashion.

The Proud Boys brawled their way into a national spotlight fighting alongside the nebula of fascist groups enlivened by Donald Trump's election in 2016, against anti-fascist groups from California to the New York island. In the aftermath of the Charlottesville riots of 2017, where the Boys were well represented, McInnes took pains to distinguish the organization from the alt-right: conservative Western chauvinists yes, but not white supremacists or anti-Semites, who are banned from his organization. It is a fact that not all Proud Boys are white; but then, neither are skinheads, whose glorification of violence and working-class mythology the Proud Boys emulate to a T. If the organization claims distinction from proud white supremacist boys of the alt-right such as Richard Spencer, to name but one, it is one of nuance more than fundamental disagreement. You should be used to it by now. Don't you have a sense of humor?

Adjacent to the Boys and other Nazi peers is a mosaic Aryan sisterhood; you will see them marching with torches, shooting paintballs and pepper spray with the worst of them, dressed in black, dressed in camo, fifty shades of white. The women of neofascism don't have a style so much as they have a commitment to the patriarchy. So, to the extent that their most visible figureheads set any fashion and appearance ideal for their sisters, what we get on the YouTube channels and Instagram accounts of the Lauren Southerns and Faith Goldys, Tomi Lahrens and Candace Owens (it takes all kinds) of the world is a peculiar mix of rhetorical smartassness and bravado and style meant to be simultaneously modest and alluring. It ain't easy being female around people who consider misogyny and domestic abuse a civilizational prerogative (surprise! Spencer verbally and physically abused his ex-wife Nina Kouprianova for years), but they try, oh lord, they try.

That a man like Spencer would gain national recognition is owing in part to the house that McInnes helped build. I don't just mean because of his hair, though it is important. Spencer made a point of discussing his undercut, which he affectuously calls a "fashy." Spencer also, it turns out, claims not to be a white supremacist but rather, following European New Right nomenclature, "an identitarian." Asked about the Nazi salutes he and his audience delivered in honor of Donald Trump's election at the annual conference of the white supremacy think tank the National Policy Institute, Spencer claimed it had been done "in a spirit of irony and exuberance." Spencer got jokes, not unlike McInnes, though arguably delivered with the pretense of reasonable discourse that makes mainstream TV happy to invite him to reasonably present his ideas for reasonable ethnic cleansing.

For a time there, Spencer was the darling of the mainstream media he purports to loathe, even as he pontificated about his dream of a white ethnostate, evoked Hitler fondly, or spouted anti-Semitic conspiracy theories. Spencer's entire strategy, one he's explained on several occasions with no qualms whatsoever, is to make fascism fashionable—and at this game, all fashions matter: the fashions that have traditionally mattered to the under-30 crowd in particular, for the same old reasons fascists have courted the youth forever, and in the same old manner, adapted to twenty-first century expectations and tastes and new fashions as well, notably piggybacking on internet subcultures. The trademark Spencer smirk is a constant reminder that an essential rhetorical accessory to his "cool" fascism is the same claim to irony perfected by the likes of McInnes.

Indeed, if Spencer made his name through such subtle acts as bellowing "Hail Trump!" in public after the 2016 election, he had been around a while, applying a playbook bound with pages taken from decades of hipsterdom: his "fashy" haircut is a multifarious signal that gestures towards current fashion, but also, always, the history of that fashion, in the hope of making fascism fashionable again. What he, McInnes and thousands of hipsters have in common is also a form of socioracial cosplay that cannot fully eschew the forms of blackface that have traditionally fed American fashions for centuries, but nevertheless attempts to offset it through reenacting a hundred years of white working-class toughs. You see it every Sunday on country roads, when 60-year-old accountants turn into rabid Hells Angels for the weekend. The impulse is not fundamentally different in Williamsburg, where young bourgeois playact as roughnecks wearing trucker hats, sleeve tattoos, undercuts like they're

Peaky Blinders and giant beards like it's 1864. If every Black man you see is a gang banger in your head, there's some logic in glorifying white gangs in turn. Spencer has gone the GQ route, but the effort is the same: in demeanor and style, he means to cosplay as his ideal of the best version of whiteness he can imagine, i.e. a Nazi trying out the stiff upper lip of a Kipling colonial officer in the dugs of a Savile Row dandy. If Kim Kardashian and other Instagram influencers' game of pretend Blackness has been granted the newfangled label of blackfishing, because blackface doesn't quite cover the twenty-first-centuryness of this specific mode of racial impersonation, should we be surprised that the Montana town Richard Spencer decided to colonize and ethnically cleanse in 2010 is named Whitefish? Think about it.

And alright. It'd be easy to look at Spencer's slow fall from flavor of the month to punched-up meme and now relative media pariah preparing his trial for domestic abuse; or at McInnes twirling his moustache at a gathering of his club and find comfort in thinking that after their fifteen minutes of fame their personal stars are somewhat dimming. Even in the 2020 presidential election season, the dynamic duo of American Nazism stayed uncharacteristically subdued. But Donald Trump's call in the first presidential debate for the shlock troops of Trumpism to "stand back and stand by" has focused popular attention on the Proud Boys and increasingly volatile protests before, during and after the electoral campaign reminded everyone that they had never left town. Their individual fates notwithstanding, Spencer and McInnes shine a light on the paths that the new fascists have paved for the past three decades in order to reach a moment like ours, where the most powerful and numerous countries of the world are all run by autocrats backed by contingents of goons who have proven capable of handling some of the strongest cultural weapons of all: fashion and irony. Their spiritual successors are legion, who have blended alternatively fascist personas that emphasize elements one might think antinomic to their political beliefs—in short, hip fascist selves. The likes of Jack Donovan, the neopagan "androphile"—a neologism he came up with in order to distinguish his brand of unabashedly Nazi gayness from what he sees as too lefty a form of gay self-assertion—or James J. O'Meara, who on top of all this presents himself as a "Green Nazi," are lurking backstage, waiting for their time at the open mic. They'll blow a kazoo in your ear and swear you've never heard anything like it before.

And you thought that goddamned hairdo was bullshit.

Chapter 4

HIPS DON'T LIE

Free Your Mind and Your Ass Will Follow.

—Parliament Funkadelic

On May 29, 2020, I sat in my living room, in COVID-19 confinement, as around the country thousands took to the streets to protest police violence. A few days earlier, white officer Derek Chauvin of the Minneapolis Police Department decided he would arrest George Floyd—an African American man whom he'd previously worked alongside of as a bouncer in local eateries—ostensibly for trying to use fake money at a local business. Assisted by three of his colleagues, Chauvin was filmed as he buried his knee into Floyd, who lay in a prone position, two other cops making sure he would not move. Chauvin did not respond to Floyd's protests that he could not breathe and maintained pressure for eight minutes and 46 seconds. The cop killed George Floyd and then went on with his business.

The US did not: days later the country erupted in massive protests. The night of May 30 saw many of them turn sour, as riot police exacerbated tensions and proved unable or unwilling to keep the peace. In Portland, Oregon, the march began peacefully in North Portland's Peninsula Park, with protesters walking south on MLK Boulevard and into downtown. There, some in the crowd aimed their anger at the Multnomah County Justice Center, and riot police moved in with flashbangs and tear gas, declaring the gathering unlawful. Small groups moved through the downtown area, breaking into and looting businesses at the Pioneer Place Mall, raising small barricades and setting them on fire, breaking windows and spray-painting walls. Stunned, mayor Ted Wheeler declared in the morning, "Portland, this is not us."

Yet undoubtedly it was, and for that matter the crowd marching peacefully while holding "Black Lives Matter" signs, much like the throngs of masked and hooded protesters of the night, looked very *Portland*: overwhelmingly young, white, skinny, favoring all-black clothes. Allies, certainly, in a city with a reputation for radical left activism and related bona fides: throughout 2019, as fascist groups organized a series of rallies across the country, they homed in on Portland precisely for that reason—and because of the city's free speech statutes. Confrontations were expected. They did happen and, predictably, Trump responded with a call to ban antifascist organizations. On May 29, the BLM march came down from the Alberta Arts District, a hub of hip and artistic activity since it was chosen for redevelopment in the 1990s, and walked past neighborhoods once inhabited by the city's African American community. If anyone felt any cognitive dissonance, it was lost in the "Black Lives Matter" chants.

Not so about a month later, when at a different BLM march across the nation, Black protestors ambled down a

Brooklyn street chanting at the many, mostly white locals on stoops or at terraces for a nice COVID brunch: "Black people used to live here! Fire, fire gentrifier!" A video about half a minute long immortalized the moment, following the marchers and catching for posterity a frieze of uncomfortable white faces. At the last table, a group of young white women can be seen timidly applauding the protestors. The video goes fairly fast. Some of the marchers appear to turn and point at them, as if to clarify that the brunchers should understand that this song was about them.

There was plenty about this video to make you feel awkward: seeing these poor patrons get hip to the consequences of their own deeds. So cringeworthy, so unfair: what if they weren't gentrifiers, huh? Maybe they did not even live in Williamsburg; what if they were just passing by and found themselves sitting there, innocent of gentrification and sincerely moved in their bodies and souls by the infectious rhythm of this chant? Does that not count? Can't we have profited from colonialism and still want its end? Shall we pay for the sins of our fathers? He that has never brunched among you, let him cast the first frittata.

As we have seen, twenty-first-century hipsterdom is convenient: every political opinion, every artistic expression is part of a menu from which to pick and create one's identity as consumer-curator. And so, politics can be mocked or claimed in turn, or both at the same time, or neither, depending on the mood and circumstantial demands. Hip gentrification is arguably the most material manifestation of hipsterdom as colonialism: evidence that the latest iteration of the cool white crowd not only builds spaces for themselves on the shoulders of people of color and the working-class, but also that they had no qualms presenting that very fact as a homage of sorts. You can hear the same arguments once used by European colonizers recycled for urban redevelopment: gentrification builds infrastructures and makes for better living. A better lifestyle, in any case. A healthier one too, why not. As hipsters settled into neighborhoods they also settled into adulthood applying to the specific issues of parenting and steady jobs the same techniques they'd applied to everything else. Hipsters-turned-adult reshape neighborhoods in the image of their preferences and needs: hipsters need hip stores, and health stores, and places to deliver on avocado toast and gluten-free goods, a neighborhood reworked from the inside out; brick-and-mortar on the outside, Amazon on the inside.

Hipsters were the shock troops of urban and cultural colonialism. Ngũgĩwa Thiong'o, the man who invented the phrase "decolonize the mind," has written that "the real aim of colonialism was to control the people's wealth: what they produced, how they produced it, and how it was distributed; to control, in other words, the entire realm of the language of life."[25] It may be hard to judge the aims of hipsterdom, but in effect its practice is well akin to this. In Brooklyn as in Albina, in London as in Austin, the rise of the hipster announced waves of gentrification that effectively priced out communities of color from historical neighborhoods, following a common pattern. After decades of real estate segregation and red-lining, practices meant to forcibly keep communities of color out of the center, the 1960s saw middle-class white inhabitants moving from cities *en masse* to the suburbs. In the wake of so-called white flight, inner city neighborhoods gained in ethnic diversity but also saw housing quality deteriorate: landlords once on hand to keep Black and brown people out of their property now allowed them to live there in lamentable conditions. Low rent attracts poor people of all sorts, and among them are down-and-out artists.

Artists play a crucial role in the grander genealogy of hip. The visual avant-garde at the start of the twentieth century were instrumental in the recognition of Black arts and artists more generally, but also in their recognition as a resource ripe for exploitation. Before these artists themselves, the first Europeans to find value in African art were self-made ethnographers traveling with colonial troops and taking advantage of collections pillaged in their bloody progress around

---

25   Ngugi wa Thiong'o, *Decolonising the Mind: the Politics of Language in African Literature* (London: J. Currey, 1986), 16.

the continent. As a few of these got busy trying to convince their snickering peers of the historical and aesthetic worth of their loot, the Picassos and Matisses, Max Ernsts and Brancusis and other visual innovators found much to admire and emulate in African arts. To them, the fact that these works had traditionally been scorned and mocked by art specialists around the Western world was part of the appeal. In turn, critics nonplussed by the avant-garde routinely mocked their apparent ignorance of the basic rules of academic art as "Negro art." To be insulted by conservatives was a badge of honor, a bohemian specialty; but in turn, the gradual recognition of African arts, driven in part by the derivative work of European modernists, led to the opening of a new market, and further pillaging.

Somewhat paradoxically, even as mainstream European culture never completely shook its scorn for Black cultures, it nevertheless admitted them as one among many colonial resources to claim and exploit. Pablo Picasso infamously pretended he was not familiar with African art when he produced the paintings of his so-called African period: irony, perhaps; and such a clever way to avoid pondering whether and to whom he might pay his dues. Like other Columbusers before him, Picasso saw Black art as something to be cut off from its roots and authors, harvested and reused as he saw fit. Having done all this hard work, he felt warranted in "picassing" all over it and calling it his. That's primitivism for you; arguably, that is also much of modernism. Think of Filippo Marinetti, who in his Futurist Manifesto—one of the founding texts of modernism—waxes lyrical about drinking mud from a "factory gutter" (nectar of the Gods for this bard of technology) only for it to remind him of the "holy black teat of [his] Sudanese nurse." Marinetti thought he might shock a bourgeois or two with this one; but then it also speaks quite straightforwardly of nurture, literally stolen out of Black people's bodies, ingested and vomited out into, and as, modern art. Primitivism in visual arts was echoed in writing and music, and goings-on in the rarefied circles of high modernism had a trickle-down effect into mainstream culture, in no small part by way of the art market. If this could sell, there had to be literal, monetary value to it, and cash ruled everything around them too.

Throughout the twentieth century, the artistic avant-garde paved the way for broader changes in tastes and aesthetics, whether or not that was the intended goal, commercial or revolutionary. We saw what this has meant for music, but we could find similar examples throughout the arts of a general movement by which Black creativity, if not always the artists themselves, was made acceptable to the broader white society through a process of dilution, adaptation and whitening. In the post-WWII period this concrete but mostly conceptual process was echoed in the physical process of gentrification. It is no easy task to make it, for an artist, and plenty of those who came looking for cheap rent in Greenwich Village in the late 1940s indeed had no money. But with awareness of the beat phenomenon came ways to cash in on it; hipsters gave way to beatniks and even squares with a slumming streak, increasingly well-off people who drove urban renovation which priced out both the original working-class population and, ironically, those of the local artists whose success or lack thereof did not make their rent. These groups moved further out to other working-class neighborhoods, and the cycle repeated itself. But worsening as it did throughout the twentieth century, this pendulum of urban migration reflected back onto the art scene in particular and culture at large. Not in a good way either.

What Sarah Schulman calls the "gentrification of the mind"—a "removal of communities of diverse classes, ethnicities, races, sexualities, languages and points of view . . . and their replacement by more homogenized groups" in cultural centers physical and metaphorical—is the engine that produced the monster that is the twenty-first-century hipster.[26] Among the unique characteristics of the twenty-first-century hipster is his conviction or pretense that his very life is, if not a piece of art, at the very least an art show to be curated, advertised, recorded, etc. This art show works by the same

26 Sarah Schulman, *Gentrification of the Mind: Witness to a Lost Imagination.* (Berkeley: University of California Press, 2012), 14.

standards of utter blandness Schulman describes: what passes for provocative material is interchangeably the radicalism or the conservatism of previous generations. It is the racist joke, that most disgustingly common product, presented as radical disruption. It is an endorsed top-bottom outlook and approach painted as edgy. Think of Francis Ford Coppola's Colonel Kurtz: the copy of a racist fictional character so full of his bloated self he thinks there is art in the mutilation of children. He'll quote T. S. Eliot at you, because of course he fucking will. Now imagine this guy thinking he's special, and either not realizing, or not caring, that the shit he is so full of also makes great fertilizer for fascism.

And yet: no one is a hipster, so no one is a gentrifier either. Nothing is serious. Still, everything has become serious, lately: blame it on the rise of American fascism. This has had an unfortunate consequence for the formerly hip: chickens have come home to roost and pick at all the outgrowths of systematic racism, including hipsters. In this moment people are demanding accountability and answers, and our hipsters think they can simply put on that coat they wear sometimes, the one that says they're anarchists sticking it to the man, not agents of, but opponents of gentrification. As Dennis Sinned shows in his in-depth study of gentrification in Williamsburg, they have convinced themselves that they are in the same position as the people whose gradual eviction has made their presence there possible; "they represent themselves as disempowered."[27] The same way no one recognizes him- or herself as a hipster, no one is a gentrifier on his or her own. Hipsterdom plays up individual uniqueness, a useful diversion in the face of gentrification and other forms of colonialism that only make sense within the frame of collective, mass action. You may be quirky, but when you're one in an army of thousands of would-be quirky middle-class white peeps moving into the same neighborhood, you should be able to consider how your individuality feeds into a whole. Black Lives Matter also makes clear, if necessary, that hipsters' cult of individuality is a lure, a diversion: it was a glaring instance in a mass movement of depoliticization whose very avowed scorn for politics made the bed for our fascist present.

Granted, some nuance gets lost in this little account of mine. As Schulman says, "key to the gentrification mentality is the replacement of complex realities with simplistic ones."[28] There are gaps in the historical record, and bias in my approach, as there are about our general understanding of what life before gentrification was like in working-class

---

27   Dennis Sinned, "Loft Lawless." *Cultural Weekly*. 21 April 2019. https://www.culturalweekly.com/loft-lawless/.

28   Schulman, 36.

neighborhoods. Reflecting on the relative dearth of information on Williamsburg between the early 1970s and the 2005 rezoning that allowed for the building of luxury condos in the area, Sinned notes "this thirty-three year gap has no shortage of persons, organizations and events worth remembering and considering."[29] Sinned's point echoes Schulman's, who describes a forgotten New York art scene burgeoning at the tail end of the 1970s made up of amateur artists who, for the most part, did not make it: they find neither commercial success nor much esteem, and many died during the AIDS epidemic. They moved into working-class neighborhoods "without ever having the need or desire to open a cute café or boutique," but meaning to produce art with "no labels or tags, no commercial intent," free and in step with their surroundings.[30] The scene (Schulman focuses on the theater) was eclectic, innovative, wild; but a modicum of success soon normalized it. Shows became increasingly formatted, copying TV standards and other structures familiar to the greater number, now their main audience, and paying customers. Theirs turned to "a destination neighborhood for

---

29   Dennis Sinned, "T/Here in Williamsburg, Part 1: Block 2399." *Cultural Weekly.* 13 September 2017. <https://www.culturalweekly.com/there-in-williamsburg-part-1-block-2399/>

30   Sarah Schulman, *Gentrification of the Mind: Witness to a Lost Imagination.* (Berkeley: University of California Press, 2012), 30; 87.

tourists who wished to drink and socialize surrounded by artists as the background scenery." The result was "an American theater profoundly complicit with *and a tool of* the dominant apparatus." Schulman and Sinned both show that gentrification doesn't just quash creativity and people. It also erases the memory of that diversity, painting the past with the same brush of homogeneity. In this light, hipsters' obsession with fashions of yore reveals its hegemonic horror: cultural colonialism also conquers the past.

Well, that was fun. And so: can we decolonize hipsters?

Good question. How do you decolonize the colonial army? Disbanding seems like a place to start, maybe, except it has long been the hipster M.O. to melt away in the greater population, Keyser Soze-style, when every doofus in the room has finally figured out what the deal was. But occupation may become less ostentatious, it may become less newsworthy, the occupying army never actually goes anywhere. The hipster moment is over, but former hipsters did not stop being so overnight. They have grown now: they've slowly retreated from the frontlines of cultural wars and taken off their uniforms, but they're not done. Many have simply turned into Nice White Parents and moved on to destroying public education or urban farming, and also repaving the streets they took over with good intentions, among other hobbies. They may be redeemable but let's not hold our breath. Worse still is that we can and should expect to see a hipster army rise again, when good things come back. So how can we avoid that?

I'll be frank: there is no easy answer here, beyond imagination. There is nothing we should strive to save in hipsterdom as we know it. This cycle of appropriation, digestion and regurgitation of cool is racism and capitalism in action. Kill capitalism and you decolonize hipsters.

There, done.

Or maybe there is a lesson to be learned from history, near and far. Maybe there is something to be gleaned from Schulman's friends, the unsung artists who moved to New York to become New Yorkers rather than to colonize, who made uncompromising art inseparable from political movements. Maybe we can start again at the beginning, at the attraction one may feel for a culture they did not grow into but nevertheless, maybe against all odds, feel sincerely partial to, whatever makes one dance to a beat, sing to a song, nod to a painting which may not totally be explained away by upbringing and social formatting, which even flies in the face of this programming. In *Mumbo Jumbo*, Ishmael Reed described "Jes' Grew," a virus which, if it "becomes pandemic it will mean the end of Civilization As We Know It."[31] Dance Apocalyptic.

31   Ishmael Reed, *Mumbo Jumbo* (New York: Atheneum, 1972), 4.

This one may hit too close to home in times of COVID
but bear with me: the virus' symptom is an uncontrollable
urge to dance that might evoke the Dancing Plague of 1518,
except Jes' Grew is an anti-plague. It does not kill, it saves;
not like the "holy black teat" Marinetti found in the mud of a
factory gutter in his feverish dreams of racist exploitation, but
like a "Black Tide of Mud" with the potential to "engulf us
all" and give the old world new life. The dance crazes of the
jazz era? That was Jes' Grew on the offensive, contaminating
the youth, a phenomenon the Wallflower Order—the age-
old secret society of whiteness—recognizes exactly for the
existential threat that it is.

Today your ass, tomorrow your mind, and then the
world: the danger of Black culture is that it may convince
people there are better things to do with oneself than whiteness. We can't have that. In the novel, the Wallflower Order
manages to thwart Jes Grew, notably by putting some stiff
academic moves on it—Black intellectuals chaperoned by
white éminence grise contain Jes' Grew with the best worded
intentions: they codify dance steps into manuals, they say
what's good and what isn't, they put some fig leaves on hump-
ing crotches and all goes back to normal. Hipsters never stood
a chance.

Or did they? There is a moment there when the virus hits
and all that matters is the act—of dancing, singing, having
sex: a politics of joy and community. Famed anarchist thinker

Emma Goldman had exactly this in mind when, responding to a comrade berating her for her tendency to slay on the dancefloor, she told him that "our Cause could not expect me to become a nun and that the movement would not be turned into a cloister. If it meant that, I did not want it. 'I want freedom, the right to self-expression, everybody's right to beautiful, radiant things.'"[32] Free your ass, your mind will follow: there, buried near the roots of hipsterdom, so close it can almost touch it, is an act more than a pose, a moment rather than an attitude, when being hip still means knowing what's up, and what's up is revolution. Under the layers of snark and self-consciousness and cool, maybe the hippening is and has always been happening.

No need to be utopian, but then, there is no reason to be cynical either. BLM protests have given us plenty of moments of rage, and a few of humor with a hefty dose of snark (Fire, fire, gentrifier!). Dare we say it's also spread a modicum of hope? It isn't that businesses and corporations and companies haven't tried to get on the BLM bandwagon and make some money off of it. The sorry spectacle of the NFL coming out in support of BLM, when protesters throughout the country emulate in their symbolic kneeling the action of former 49ers quarterback Colin Kaepernick is beyond pathetic, and it is

32 Emma Goldman. *Living My Life* (New York: Cosimo Classics, 2011; 1931), 56.

but one striking example among many of tone-deaf corporations trying to bet the bank on Black, if you'll allow me. Some were more subtle and clever than the NFL, yet overall these initiatives were met with a healthy dose of skepticism, as if these attempts at appropriation—that favorite tool of hipsters—were no longer so efficient.

For decades, *Vice* magazine's "Dos and Don'ts" section proposed snapshots of random people taken on the streets of North American cities captioned by the forever troll, Gavin McInnes, in the merciless misanthrope hip style he, and this magazine item, did so much to popularize. The section showcased the cool and not-so-cool, the extravagant and the ridiculous, blurring praise and insult, admiration and mockery. It also set standards of hipster self-representation: with every single sartorial choice up to be dissected, skewered and put on display for all to see, one should always expect scrutiny. The internet played a crucial role in spreading these rules and expectations, with sites like the defunct Tumblr "Look at That Fucking Hipster" making widely accessible the stylings of an ever-updated roster of random hipsters. Thus, hipsters themselves could now take the place of the musicians, artists who traditionally served as their models or inspiration.

In 2010, a year after LATFH first appeared online, a new app named Instagram was introduced, harkening the age of the influencer, rising from the ashes of hip. Denizens of Instagram, influencers offer up their lives to us mere mortals in packaged, curated streams of delightfully staged portraits replete with product placements. Not every selfie-conscious Instagrammer is or was a hipster, but the narrow focus typical of the platform owes something to these cool forebears. Seemingly self-plucked from nothingness, these women and men took the dynamic of "Dos and Don'ts" and LATFH and flipped it: where these columns forcibly stepped into the moments of strangers, now strangers invited whoever might be interested to satisfy their curiosity and be on every street with them, all the time, consuming their lives as an endless series of snapshots. Looking at them real quick might as easily give the illusion of motion, sincerity and intent, as reveal the editing, artifice, and shallowness.

Instagram spread the end point of the hipster offensive: lifestyle-as-style, the pretense that every aspect of one's life could and should be evidence and demonstration, if not of actual taste, of how to make things look tasteful. Look at my brunch; maybe I made it (not), maybe I had it at a brand new restaurant no one yet has heard about, but here it is, plated like life is a cooking TV show, looking flawless in my Juno filter. With Instagram, your entire life can be a glossy magazine, and you can be its perpetual star. The question of the gaze and its gender is also turned upside down. The grammar of Instagram would make one simultaneously object and subject; offered up to the world for admiration, impervious to scorn, in full control of one's self-representation. If fashion always gave us a way to look at people through a glass of their own choosing—if not your own making—Instagram turn us to a hall of mirrors, endlessly reflecting surface off surface. However little makeup one wears in photos, however much fat one pinches, there is no authenticity onscreen but perhaps in the curating itself. Instagram made hipsterdom meta.

But that turns out to be a problem. Because for all that they might steel themselves against mockery, influencers mean to be taken seriously. So they'll endorse conscious hashtags and causes *du jour* as easily as they'll flaunt their perfect hairdo, and for the same reasons: because it demonstrates their unique worth. #Kony2012, y'all.

Influencers saw opportunity in BLM protests, chances in New York, Seattle, LA, what have you, to capture wary but committed photographic evidence of their commitment to the cause. Thus "social media influencer/model" Kris Schatzel, hair tousled just so, sheer black dress flowing just enough, posed on a Los Angeles sidewalk, protesters forming the backdrop as she held a small whiteboard inscribed with the words "Black Lives Matter," staring intently, seriously into the camera. This ain't no joke! This is 2020, and someone managed to film Schatzel and her assistant as they staged the moment. The video they released was entitled "Stop treating protests like Coachella pt 17." Indeed, Schatzel was not the only influencer caught using protest movements like her own personal soda commercial. Complete with the mocking gasps and snarky commentary of its creator, the video was viewed by millions of people, many of whom derided Schatzel, calling out her callousness for using the movement as an opportunity for self-promotion. This, arguably, was a testimony that the times were a-changin.' In a subsequent post, Schatzel non-apologized for trying to "spread the message." But a quick look at Instagram these days will show that the accounts actually spreading the message tend to espouse a wholly different approach to social networking, often eschewing personal publicity to focus on events. Imagine that.

Instagram belongs to Facebook, and Facebook belongs to Zuckerberg, and Zuckerberg has had no qualms cashing in on the rise of internet-fueled fascism. But still, the tool here is doing something it was not quite designed to do, and its users are acting in ways they were not expected to. Black IG and Black Twitter are the tips of Blacktivist icebergs pushing the current wave, a collective that has so far managed to eschew figureheads and spokespeople and heroes, showed savvy in navigating media and social networks and stayed focused in the face of extreme brutality and terrorizing state tactics. We can imagine the worst is yet to come. Meanwhile though, we have reasons to hope that things can be different. It seems concerned white participants have been reflecting on their own involvement in white supremacy and the best ways they can be allies in this struggle.

This is when we talk about beards again.

In Chapter 1, I evoked the twenty-first-century hipster as an apocalyptic negative of the bearded abolitionist John Brown; the latter had announced the Civil War, the former this moment of crisis and whatever else might come afterward. But there, perhaps, is also the closest one can get to decolonizing hipsters. If white privilege expresses itself in "the artful shirking of human responsibility in the face of ongoing injustice," its epitome, its quintessentially white pinnacle was hipsterdom, or dedicatedly approaching all facets of human experience—including social and political matters—as consumer products.[33] Committing to fighting injustice is a bit harder than growing facial hair, but the two have this in common that they can have world-changing consequences. A few years ago, in the very pages of *Vice*, the erstwhile hipster Bible, Carvell Wallace imagined dark-humoredly the possibility that hipsters might go all the way and appropriate "from the rest of the world... our total refusal to treat our lives as a theoretical joke."[34] But he knows well that decolonization takes more than passive consumption. So I call upon you, beardmongers of good will, who perhaps got into cool

---

33   Patrice Evans, "Hip-Hop & Hipsterism," *What Was the Hipster?: A Sociological Investigation*. Mark Greif, Kathleen Ross, Dayna Tortorici eds. (New York: n+1 Foundation, 2010), 103.

34   Wallace.

but not into racism and maybe find yourselves currently beating the pavement, or wanting to, or in support of it all. There is a way, and it does not require you solve the impossible problem of figuring out how to buy ethnic facepaint now that COVID-19 will most likely cancel the next Afropunk festival. Close to thirty years ago, the late Noel Ignatiev and John Garvey (incidentally, a labor activist born and raised on the streets of pre-hip Brooklyn) started the journal *Race Traitor*, bearing the bold motto: "Treason to whiteness is loyalty to humanity." The editorial of their first issue set their goals in these terms: "The white race is a club, which enrolls certain people at birth, without their consent, and brings them up according to its rules . . . *Race Traitor* aims to dissolve the club, to break it apart, to explode it."[35] The authors were describing a moment much like the present one, in the aftermath of the Los Angeles uprising following the beating of Rodney King at the hands of LAPD officers as one when white people of goodwill, "neither deeply nor consciously committed to white supremacy" saw their usual apathy shaken.[36] What, they asked, "if enough of those who looked white broke the rules of the club to make the cops doubt their ability to

---

35   "Editorial: Abolish the white race—by any means necessary." *Race Traitor* 1 (Winter 1993), 2.

36   Ibid., 4.

recognize a white person merely by looking at him or her . . . ?
And if the police, the courts, and the authorities in general
were to start spreading around discriminately the treatment
they normally reserve for people of color, how would the rest
of the so-called whites react?"[37] Ignatiev and Garvey were
not so bold as to provide an answer. Today, a long while after
1993, we may be starting to get one.

That's it, then, your directive to undo the hipster:
embrace the John Brown under the beard, and the portent
of war beyond it—not a war against people, but a war against
whiteness. Decolonized hipsters will not just get up and follow Black marchers or drummers in protests, shake their hips
to their beat and call it a day. They won't just adapt their forebears' familiar practices to current politics. They will have
to also emulate those predecessors they have forgotten, the
unsung doers, the artists and workers and unionists that once
peopled the streets where nitro cold brew now flows, those
forgotten people who wittingly or not chipped at the walls of
the whites-only club.

The decolonized hipster is a race traitor: see if you can
find anything cooler than that.

37   Ibid., 4-5.

ACKNOWLEDGMENTS

I would never have finished this without the help and support of Marlene Daut, Anne Eller, Tao Goffe, Moura McGovern, Bhakti Shringarpure, Chelsea Stieber, Molly Petersen and Sarah Wasserman. At different points in the grueling path towards completion of this volume they were kind enough to read drafts, question poor judgment and choices, veto bad jokes and second better ones, suggest clarifications, and illuminate paths. Eternal thanks to all of you brilliant people.

GRÉGORY PIERROT is a professor at the University of Connecticut at Stamford. He is the author of *The Black Avenger in Atlantic Culture*, co-editor of the forthcoming *An Anthology of Haitian Revolutionary Fictions*, and co-host of the *Decolonize That!* webcast series.

9 781682 193174